Fodor's

25 Best

KRAKOW

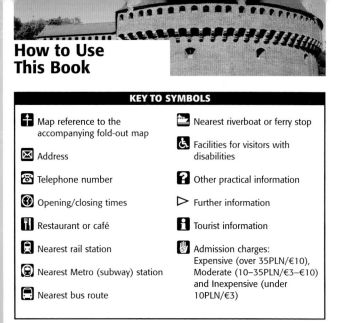

How to Use
This Book

KEY TO SYMBOLS	
✚ Map reference to the accompanying fold-out map	🛥 Nearest riverboat or ferry stop
✉ Address	♿ Facilities for visitors with disabilities
☎ Telephone number	❓ Other practical information
🕐 Opening/closing times	▷ Further information
🍴 Restaurant or café	ℹ Tourist information
🚆 Nearest rail station	✋ Admission charges: Expensive (over 35PLN/€10), Moderate (10–35PLN/€3–€10) and Inexpensive (under 10PLN/€3)
Ⓜ Nearest Metro (subway) station	
🚌 Nearest bus route	

This guide is divided into four sections
● Essential Krakow: An introduction to the city and tips on making the most of your stay.
● Krakow by Area: We've broken the city into six areas, and recommended the best sights, shops, entertainment venues, nightlife and restaurants in each one. Suggested walks help you to explore on foot.
● Where to Stay: The best hotels, whether you're looking for luxury, budget or something in between.
● Need to Know: The info you need to make your trip run smoothly, including getting about by public transport, weather tips, emergency phone numbers and useful websites.

Navigation In the Krakow by Area chapter, we've given each area its own color, which is also used on the locator maps throughout the book and the map on the inside front cover.

Maps The fold-out map with this book is a comprehensive street plan of Krakow. The grid on this fold-out map is the same as the grid on the locator maps within the book. We've given grid references within the book for each sight and listing.

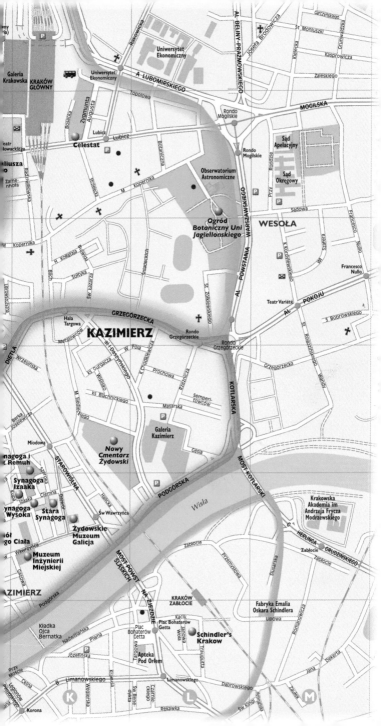

Contents

ESSENTIAL KRAKOW	4–18
Introducing Krakow	4–5
A Short Stay in Krakow	6–7
Top 25	8–9
Shopping	10–11
Shopping by Theme	12
Krakow by Night	13
Where to Eat	14
Where to Eat by Cuisine	15
Top Tips For...	16–18

KRAKOW BY AREA	19–106
RYNEK GŁÓWNY	**20–38**
Area map	22–23
Sights	24–34
Walk	35
Shopping	36
Entertainment and Nightlife	37
Where to Eat	38

WITHIN THE PLANTY	39–58
Area map	40–41
Sights	42–54
Walk	55
Shopping	56
Entertainment and Nightlife	57
Where to Eat	58

WAWEL HILL	59–68
Area map	60–61
Sights	62–67
Where to Eat	68

KAZIMIERZ	69–84
Area map	70–71
Sights	72–79
Walk	80–81
Shopping	82
Entertainment and Nightlife	83
Where to Eat	84

BEYOND THE PLANTY	85–96
Area map	86–87
Sights	88–95
Where to Eat	96

FARTHER AFIELD	97–106
Area map	98–99
Sights	100–104
Excursions	105
Entertainment and Nightlife	106
Where to Eat	106

WHERE TO STAY	107–112
Introduction	108
Budget hotels	109
Mid-range hotels	110–111
Luxury hotels	112

NEED TO KNOW	113–125
Planning Ahead	114–115
Getting There	116–117
Getting Around	118–119
Essential Facts	120–121
Language	122–123
Timeline	124–125

CONTENTS

Introducing Krakow

Krakow has a great tradition of hospitality, and has been welcoming visitors since the Middle Ages. Its old buildings are beautifully restored, yet as a university city it has moved with the times, kept young and vibrant by its lively student population.

There's more than one Krakow to experience and you can see many different faces of the city in a day, since it's an easy place to negotiate. Its attractions are concentrated in the relatively small area of the Old Town, whose streets have barely changed since the 13th century. It's all walkable, but be prepared for lots of stairs. Cafés, restaurants, bars and clubs occupy every corner and floor, from the cellars to the attics to the courtyards. It's one of the thrills of Krakow life to push open an ancient wooden door and hear the very latest band pulsing up from below. Alternatively, you can take in a classical concert in a magnificent baroque church.

Maybe you just want to have a good time in the Old Town. No problem—you'll find reasonably priced accommodations, food and entertainment, and English is widely understood. Yet, while tourism is important to Krakow, the city has in no way surrendered its own identity to it. As a former capital of Poland—a country that has been invaded time and again and come back fighting—it is fiercely proud of its traditions.

One of the latest areas to revive is Kazimierz, the former Jewish district. Its people were annihilated in World War II, yet their culture is again being celebrated. Spend the evening listening to *klezmer* music or sitting in one of Kazimierz's bars. Across the bridge is up-and-coming Podgórze, once the site of the Jewish ghetto, today home to three new museums (including an exhibition in the former Schindler factory), some great restaurants and fashionable cafés.

You don't have to go to any museums or art galleries—though Krakow has many—to absorb the soul of this very varied city.

FACTS AND FIGURES

- Population: 769,000
- Annual number of visitors: 12 million
- Size of Rynek Główny: 210m x 212m (229 x 231 yards), the largest medieval square in Europe
- Number of churches: 119
- Number of bars: 400-plus in the Old Town alone

MERCHANT CITY

Krakow's early wealth came from its location on the main trade routes between Europe and Asia, and the Baltic and the Mediterranean. Then, as now, it was a cosmopolitan city. The salt mined nearby at Wieliczka and Bochnia made Krakow's grand families rich and paid for its beautiful buildings.

LUCKY TATAR

The image of the Lajkonik, a medieval Tatar on a gaily caparisoned steed, is almost as common as fluffy dragons in Krakow. Every May or June, a man dressed as Lajkonik leads a parade through the city, touching spectators with his golden mace to bring luck for the year and receiving small gifts of money in return.

POPE'S CRADLE

Krakow is the city that raised the first Polish pope. Karol Wojtyła lived here as a student of literature, worker, actor, poet and priest. As bishop and archbishop, he was the students' favorite; as John Paul II, he drew the crowds to celebrate Mass on Krakow's Błonia fields—2 million on the occasion of his last visit, in 2002.

A Short Stay in Krakow

DAY 1

Morning Breakfast in one of the cafés in Rynek Główny—Main Square—and you'll see some of the best city sights from your table.

Mid-morning Walk up the Royal Route of ul. Grodzka to **Wawel Hill** (▷ 64–65) and the cathedral, where the kings of Poland and some of its heroes are laid to rest, then tour the castle. After taking in the view over the Vistula River toward the futuristic **Manggha Japanese Center** (▷ 95), make your way down to the riverside **Dragon's Lair** (▷ 66) and get close to the Smok, who breathes real fire.

Lunch In summer, eat on one of the floating restaurants moored here or cook your own Polish sausage at an open-air barbecue restaurant. In winter, make you way back to ul. św. Anny and the popular **Chimera Salad Bar** (▷ 58).

Afternoon Back in the Rynek Główny, **St. Mary's Church** (▷ 26–27) is a must-see, after which you can examine the fine facades of the **Kamienice** (▷ 25), the noblemen's houses that line the square. If you have the energy, finish in the **Sukiennice** (▷ 30–31) in the center of the square, whose stalls sell every kind of souvenir.

Dinner In a city that has welcomed visitors for centuries, one restaurant takes the prize. Eat at **Wierzynek** (▷ 29, 38), which has been feeding guests since 1364 and has a fine view of the square and the little church of **St. Adalbert's** (▷ 33).

Evening If you're a clubber, make for **Prozak** (▷ 57) or the slightly less sophisticated **Jazz Rock Café** (▷ 57). Quieter souls can take in a film at **Cracow Cinema Center Ars** (▷ 57) or just have a nightcap.

DAY 2

Morning Take a stroll in the Planty before breakfast and see students rushing to their lectures—beware of cyclists. Wherever your stroll finishes, turn in toward the center of town for breakfast and you'll find a choice of atmospheric cafés in the side streets.

Mid-morning Go underground to explore the depths of Krakow's history in **Rynek Underground** (the vaults beneath the Market Square, ▷ 31). The entrance is in the Sukiennice.

Lunch Try something typically Polish at an old-fashioned "milk bar," an inexpensive self-service café that would originally just have served up glasses of milk but now offers traditional home-cooked dishes. **Bar Mleczny Pod Temidą** (▷ 58) is a good choice.

Afternoon Work off your meal with a 20-minute walk to Kazimierz, the former Jewish quarter. Or be lazy and take a tram. Start at plac Wolnica by visiting the **Ethnographic Museum** (▷ 72–73) before exploring the synagogues, or walk down ul. Miodowa to ul. Szeroka, the hub of most of the Jewish restaurants and historic buildings.

Dinner After maybe browsing for books or antiques or dropping in on a lecture at the **Galicia Jewish Museum** (▷ 77), shake off the seriousness at one of the many restaurants that features *klezmer* music. They serve a nostalgic kind of Jewish cuisine to accompany the uplifting tunes.

Evening The night is always young in Kazimierz. Begin a café crawl at **Alchemia** (▷ 83)—there may be a good band on at its adjoining Music Hall. Then continue around **Plac Nowy** (▷ 74) and the streets leading off it, according to taste.

Top 25

ESSENTIAL KRAKOW TOP 25

▶ ▶ ▶

Auschwitz-Birkenau
▷ **100–101** The former Nazi concentration camp is now a memorial.

Żydowskie Muzeum Galicja ▷ **77** This fine museum is devoted to the Jewish heritage of Galicia.

Synagoga i Cmentarz Remuh ▷ **76** Remuh Synagogue and Cemetery was founded for a celebrated rabbi and still holds services today.

Sukiennice ▷ **30–31** Stalls galore sell jewelry and souvenirs in Krakow's ancient Cloth Hall.

Stara Synagoga ▷ **75** The Old Synagogue is testament to the rich history of Jewish culture in the city.

Smocza Jama ▷ **66** Symbol of the city, Krakow's dragon still belches fire outside the Dragon's Lair.

Schindler's Krakow ▷ **92–93** Over the river in the district of Podgórze you'll find memories of Krakow's Nazi-run ghetto.

Restauracja Wierzynek ▷ **29** The Wierzynek Restaurant launched with a royal banquet in 1364.

Collegium Maius ▷ **42–43** The Museum of the Jagiellonian University, Poland's oldest university.

Plac Nowy ▷ **74** This square is the site of a daytime market and the heart of Kazimierz's nightlife.

Hejnał ▷ **24** A real bugler marks the hour from the top of St. Mary's Watchtower.

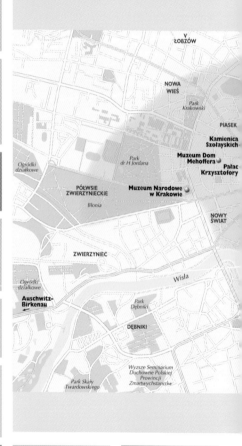

Pałac Krzysztofory ▷ **28** St. Christopher's Palace houses the Historical Museum of Krakow.

Jama Michalika ▷ **44** This café was the haunt of Krakow's artistic society at the turn of the 20th century.

Kamienice ▷ **25** These grand noblemen's houses in the Old Town give Krakow its medieval character.

Kamienica Szołayskich ▷ **45** The Wyspiański exhibition here celebrates the Krakow-born artist.

Katedra Wawelska ▷ **62–63** Wawel Cathedral is the country's most important church.

Kopalnia Soli Wieliczka ▷ **102–103** Wieliczka Salt Mine has jaw-dropping underground caverns.

Kościół Franciszkanów ▷ **46–47** The Franciscan Church is noted for its beautiful stained glass.

Kościół Mariacki ▷ **26–27** St. Mary's Church is a Gothic masterpiece.

Muzeum Dom Mehoffera ▷ **88–89** Mehoffer's House was home to one of Krakow's leading artists.

Muzeum Etnograficzne ▷ **72–73** The city's Ethnographic Museum.

Muzeum Książąt Czartoryskich ▷ **48–49** Currently being restored, but Da Vinci's *Lady with an Ermine* usually resides here.

Pałac Królewski na Wawelu ▷ **64–65** Wawel Castle was the seat of Poland's kings for centuries.

Pałac Biskupa Erazma Ciołka ▷ **50** This palace houses the Museum of Art of Old Poland.

Muzeum Narodowe w Krakowie ▷ **90–91** The National Museum holds Polish modern art.

Shopping

For centuries, the wealth created by the nearby salt mines enabled Krakow's gentry to buy silks from the East and import art and architects from Italy. Today, much of the retail trade in the Old Town comes from tourism, yet so far Krakow has resisted the usual mass-produced souvenirs (the stalls at the Dragon's Cave excepted) and sell a good selection of attractive, locally produced craftwork.

Amber

Called *bursztyn* in Polish, amber is everywhere in Poland and the Baltic states. Since it consists of the solidified resin of prehistoric pine trees, it is not as hard as some gemstones, and it feels warm against the skin. Most of the amber you will see on sale is an opaque honey-yellow or a transparent tea color. Each piece is unique; some may contain an insect or a small fern, trapped in the amber as it solidified. Always check that you are buying genuine amber—the inexpensive pendants on sale in souvenir shops may well be plastic. Do not buy for investment unless you are an expert.

Jewelry

Poland has a strong design tradition and this is particularly true of the jewelry you'll see on sale in the Old Town. Usually in silver with gemstones or amber but often in acrylic, too, pieces make a unique memento.

SHOPPING MALLS

If you are suffering withdrawal symptoms from the big-city shopping experience, Krakow now has plenty of places to spend your złoty. Packed with international retail chains, Galeria Krakowska stands conveniently next to the railway station and is the city's most accessible mall. If you are willing to travel farther afield, Krakow Serenada shopping mall is a short bus and tram ride northeast along Bora Komorowskiego, while Galeria Kazimierz lies to the southeast of the Old Town on ul. Podgórska and is closer to the center.

Clockwise from top left: Jewelry set with different shades of amber; flavored vodka; clothing boutique; handmade lace;

Food and Drink

You'll find many varieties of vodka on sale (▷ 13). Not quite so strong is *miód pitny*, a kind of mead. Polish chocolates are a little different from their Western European and American counterparts. See a good range in Wawel or Wedel, both in the Rynek Główny, and in Karmello in Floriańska nearby. Plums and praline are popular fillings.

Arts and Crafts

You can buy wooden trinket boxes and carved wooden items, usually in a naïve style that is typical of the countryside around Krakow. Small stained-glass hangings are pretty. Some of the embroidered blouses that are part of the regional folk garb are wearable without the rest of the costume, and linen tablecloths and napkins are good value, as are leather goods. Also very practical are sheepskin gloves and slippers. Something you don't find in many other places is armor. You'll see swords, chainmail and helmets all on sale—some authentic, others not.

Christmas Market

Stalls crowd the main square for the month of December, and mulled wine and grilled snacks are on sale to help you get in the mood to buy. Mostly the goods are similar to what's available year-round, but with the emphasis on gifts. The Christmas Market is one of the most magical experiences in Krakow, especially in the snow.

STREET EATS

Every street in Krakow's Old Town seems to have a stall selling *obwarzanki*—tasty pretzels sprinkled with poppy or sesame seeds, and ideal to nibble with a beer in the sunshine. They are believed to be the predecessors of the famous New York bagels, brought there by immigrants from Krakow. You'll also see sellers of *oscypek*, squeaky sheep's milk cheese. Usually smoked, it's traditionally made in the Tatra Mountains. In winter, it's grilled over braziers and sold hot during the Christmas market.

jars of spicy pickles; a stall selling icons in the Cloth Hall; crystal wine glasses; colorful wooden toys

Shopping by Theme

Small shops with a strong, individual character are still common in Krakow, but you'll find your favorite labels are well represented too, especially in the big shopping centers just outside the Old Town. For more details, see the listings in Krakow by Area.

Antiques/Curios
Antyki Józefa (▷ 82)
Antyki Sosenko (▷ 36)
Galeria Osobliwości ESTE (▷ 56)
Galeria Szalom (▷ 82)
Szpeje (▷ 82)

Arts and Crafts
Dekor Art (▷ 56)
Galeria Przedmiotu AB (▷ 36)
Galerie D'Art Naïf (▷ 82)

Books and Media
Austeria (▷ 82)
Cracow Poster Gallery (▷ 56)
Galicia Jewish Museum (▷ 77)
High Synagogue (▷ 79)
Księgarnia Kurant (▷ 36)

Clothing
Click (▷ 56)
Mapaya (▷ 82)
Zebra (▷ 36)

Food and Drink
Karmello (▷ 56)
Krakowski Kredens (▷ 56)
Produkty Benedyktyńskie (▷ 82)
Szambelan (▷ 36)
Wawel (▷ 36)

Glass
Polskie Szkło (▷ 56)

Jewelry
Blazko Kindery (▷ 82)
Diament (▷ 56)
Galeria Ora (▷ 56)

Malls
Galeria Kazimierz (▷ 82)
Pasaż 13 (▷ 36)

Markets
Plac Nowy (▷ 74, panel, 82)
Stary Kleparz (▷ panel, 96)

Souvenirs/Gifts
Lu'lua (▷ 82)
Sukiennice (▷ 36)

Krakow by Night

Despite the vast range and number of bars in the Old Town, Krakow nightlife is not only about drinking. As a student city, Krakow has its share of clubs, but film is very popular here too, with many cinemas showing movies in the original language. Music of every contemporary genre pulses through the cellars in the Old Town, while lovers of classical music can enjoy many beautiful venues.

Relaxed Summers

In summer, most cafés, bars and restaurants have outside tables and the fine buildings in the Old Town are dramatically lit at night. Rynek Główny is filled with diners and drinkers, and the lack of traffic, apart from the occasional horse-drawn carriage, means you can hear the buzz of conversation. In general, it's safe to wander within the Planty in the evenings. Kazimierz is a little more edgy but things are generally good-humored and peaceful.

Winter Retreats

When winter arrives, the cellar bars and thick stone walls of the venerable buildings really come into their own. Doors are kept closed to hold the heat in, so push at that 14th-century slab of wood studded with iron and you may find a restaurant with a roaring fire or a jazz band working up a sweat. No one wants to venture back out into the cold, which may be how the Krakow tradition of staying open "until the last guest" began.

From top: A jazz concert; juggling fire; a Polish band on stage; a jazz club; a hot-air balloon on Rynek Główny

---

VODKA LORE

Learning about vodka can be an entertainment in itself, and bar staff will be happy to teach you. Usually distilled from rye and widely accepted as the world's purest, Polish vodka comes in various flavors, but until you see a Krakow bar you may not have appreciated quite how many. Żubrówka, or bison-grass vodka, and cherry-flavored Wiśniówka are two of the most common. Wyborowa, which means "exquisite," is a good brand.

Where to Eat

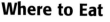

The stereotype of Polish food is dumplings and sausage, and it's true that you may be offered well-seasoned lard, rather than butter, for your bread. But Krakow is now full of excellent restaurants serving lighter dishes made from local ingredients as well as traditional, more hearty fare, which disprove the old travelers' tales.

When to Eat
In Krakow, each establishment makes its own rules. The smarter and more ambitious restaurants will keep normal restaurant hours, opening for lunch and dinner only. Most of the other places begin serving by 9am, with some cafés starting as early as 7am, and will stay open until the small hours.

Where to Eat
Some cake shops also serve savory snacks and sandwiches. Some cafés serve only tea, coffee and their home-cooked cheesecake; others serve wine and beer but not vodka and have a more extensive menu of snacks. Nearly all bars will have some kind of sandwich or other snack to help line your stomach, while some of the more atmospheric cellar bars have restaurant areas. In summer, tables spill onto the streets and many places open a secret garden—look for the sign *ogródek*—which can be anything from a delightful tree-shaded former monastery plot to the inner courtyard of a grand town house, overhung by upstairs balconies. You'll find the greatest concentration of cafés and restaurants in the Old Town within the Planty and in Kazimierz.

From top: Alchemia bar; Chata restaurant; a pavement café; Chimera Salad Bar

---

TIPPING

Drink and meal prices are still pretty reasonable by European standards, so tipping is not a painful process. Leaving your bartender some change and rounding up the taxi fare to the nearest 5 zloty is common practice. Tipping in restaurants is discretionary—if you were happy with the service, 10 percent will be a nice gesture.

Where to Eat by Cuisine

There are places to eat to suit all tastes and budgets in Krakow. On this page they are listed by cuisine. For a more detailed description of each venue, see Krakow by Area.

Asian
Youmiko Sushi (▷ 84)

Fine Dining
Copernicus (▷ 58)

Historic Rooms
Hawełka (▷ 38)
Wentzl (▷ 38)
Wierzynek (▷ 38)

European
Corse (▷ 58)
Euskadi (▷ 96)
Karczma Sabała (▷ 106)
Nolio (▷ 84)
Petite France (▷ 58)
Plaża Kraków (▷ 96)
Restauracja Szara (▷ 38)
Smak Ukraiński (▷ 68)
Zakładka (▷ 96)

Jewish Food
Awiw (▷ 84)
Klezmer-Hois (▷ 84)
Once Upon A Time In
Kazimierz (▷ 84)

Light Bites
Aquarius (▷ 68)
Bal (▷ 96)
Café Szafé (▷ 96)
Dynia (▷ 96)
Europejska (▷ 38)
Kawiarnia Pod Basztą
(▷ 68)
Kawiarnia Ratuszowa
(▷ 38)

Typically Polish
Bar Mleczny Pod Temidą
(▷ 58)
Cechowa (▷ 58)
Chata (▷ 96)

Chata Zbójnicka (▷ 106)
Gościniec Pod Zamkiem
(▷ 84)
Gruszka Nova (▷ 58)
Karczma Czarci Jar
(▷ 106)
Karczma Obrochtówka
(▷ 106)
Kawaleria (▷ 58)
Kuchnia U Doroty
(▷ 84)
Pod Baranem (▷ 68)
Pod Smoczą Jamą
(▷ 68)
Pod Wawelem (▷ 68)
Wesele (▷ 38)

Veggie-Friendly
Café Camelot (▷ 58)
Chimera Salad Bar
(▷ 58)
Nova Krova (▷ 84)

Top Tips For...

These great suggestions will help you tailor your ideal visit to Krakow, no matter how you choose to spend your time. Each sight or listing has a fuller write-up elsewhere in the book.

KEEPING YOUR CHILDREN HAPPY

Krakow Zoo (▷ 106), in the middle of Las Wolski, has big-cat breeding programs.
The Park Jordana (▷ 94) children's playground is next to Błonia fields.

A WALK IN THE PARK

Stroll in the Botanic Gardens (▷ 95). If wet, there are greenhouses to explore.
Błonia fields (▷ 94) has enough space for everyone in Krakow, including you and your kite.
Greening the city in summer, and giving breathing space in winter, the Planty (▷ 55) is a park for all seasons.

HISTORY'S DARK SIDE

Ulica Pomorska (▷ 95), a museum of Krakow during World War II, is housed in a former Gestapo building.
The memorial museums at Auschwitz-Birkenau (▷ 100–101) are a powerful reminder of the horrors of the Holocaust.
A simple cross commemorates the murder of thousands of Polish officers at Katyń (▷ 52).

CLASSICAL MUSIC

Within the exuberantly decorated Teatr Słowackiego (▷ 54) you can see visiting artists and companies as well as homegrown opera.
Poland's biggest philharmonic orchestra, the Filharmonia (▷ 57), is joined by the best international musicians.
Many of Krakow's churches, such as SS. Peter and Paul (▷ 52), host regular performances in beautiful surroundings.
Krakow Festival Office organizes excellent classical music festivals throughout the year.

Clockwise from top: an outdoor performance at the jazz festival in July; walking by the river below Wawel Hill;

DANCING AT NIGHT

Hedonists shake it all about until the early hours every night at Jazz Rock Café (▷ 57).
Always wanted to shimmy with Lenin? Pub Propaganda (▷ 83) is the place.
Get your glad rags on if you want to join the beautiful people at Prozak (▷ 57).

ALL THAT JAZZ

The cellar of the intimate Harris Piano Jazz Bar (▷ 37) is usually crammed full of aficionados.
Spreading out to various venues from the Piwnica Pod Baranami (▷ 33), the July festival is the highspot of the year.
Alchemia's Music Hall (▷ 83) off the main bar hosts jazz concerts with international stars.

TAKING THE LONG VIEW

The old, imposing fort of the Barbakan, just inside the northern edge of the Planty, offers fine views from its upper galleries (▷ 50).
Bring a złoty to look through the telescopes when you get to the top of the Town Hall Tower (▷ 34).
A short hike or bus and tram ride out of the city will bring you to the view from Kościuszko Mound (▷ 104).

ARCHITECTURE OLD AND NEW

The uncompromisingly modern Manggha Japanese Center (▷ 95) provides an antidote to Krakow Gothic.
St. Adalbert's (▷ 33) in the Rynek Główny is one of the city's oldest and smallest churches, founded in the 11th century.
The fin-de-siècle flourishes of the Teatr Słowackiego (▷ 54) were influenced by the Paris Opera.

STAYING ON A SHOESTRING

Piano Guest House (▷ 109) is a simple but comfortable home from home near the main rail station.
Cybulskiego Guest Rooms (▷ 109) offer mini apartments just outside the Planty.

St. Adalbert's church; ornate interior of the Teatr Słowackiego; the Planty; Krakow Zoo

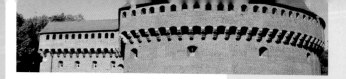

CAFÉ SOCIETY

Don't miss Jama Michalika, an artists' haunt from a century ago (▷ 44).

Quirky, cozy Café Camelot (▷ 58) is filled with naive art and is an atmospheric place to have breakfast.

At Singer in Kazimierz (▷ 83), you can drink your coffee at a table made out of an old sewing machine.

To experience the Kazimierz bohemian vibe, try Alchemia at Plaz Nowy (▷ 83), with its candlelit Gothic interior.

SLEEPING IN THE LAP OF LUXURY

You can count the stars from the rooftop rooms at the Hotel Copernicus (▷ 112).

Or count the famous people who have stayed at the venerable Pod Różą hotel (▷ 112)—such as Balzac, Liszt and Tsar Alexander I.

For boutique chic, sleep in the history-rich Hotel Maltański (▷ 112).

HISTORIC CHURCHES

The twin towers of the Romanesque St. Andrew's (▷ 50–51) withstood the Tatar invasion of 1241.

Sadly the unfortunate bugler (▷ 24) in the tower of St. Mary's Church was caught by a Tatar arrow.

Wawel Cathedral (▷ 62–63) has been the setting for almost all Polish coronations.

JEWISH CULTURE

Visit the Galicja Jewish Museum (▷ 77) to find out how the heritage continues.

Dine at Klezmer-Hois (▷ 84) to hear some of the best *klezmer* bands.

Don't miss the Schindler's factory (▷ 93), part of the Historical Museum, which tells the story of Krakow's Jewish population during World War II.

In summer, enjoy the Jewish Culture Festival (▷ 114) with wonderful artists from all over the world, which has been held every June in Kazimierz since 1988.

From top: Café society; Hotel Copernicus; St. Andrew's church; music at Klezmer-Hois

Krakow by Area

Rynek Główny 20–38

Within the Planty 39–58

Wawel Hill 59–68

Kazimierz 69–84

Beyond the Planty 85–96

Farther Afield 97–106

Rynek Główny

Laid out in 1257 and the largest market square in medieval Europe, Rynek Główny is where all Krakow meets to relax, buy flowers, celebrate or protest. From 1320, when citizens first gathered to pay homage to the king on the square, it has been at the heart of city life.

Top 25

Hejnał **24**

Kamienice **25**

Kościół Mariacki **26**

Pałac Krzysztofory **28**

Restauracja Wierzynek **29**

Sukiennice **30**

More to See **32**

Walk **35**

Shopping **36**

Entertainment and Nightlife **37**

Where to Eat **38**

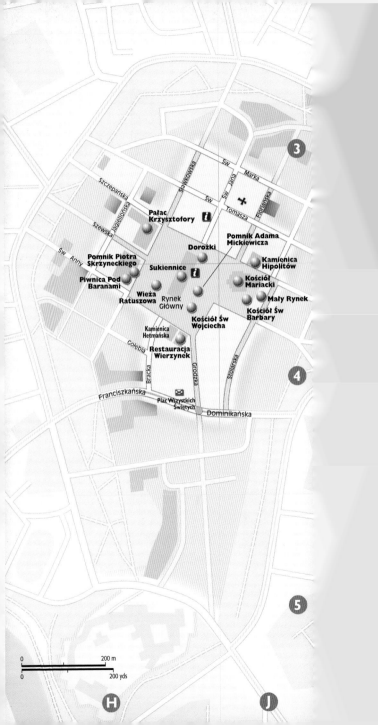

Hejnał

The bugle call (left); St. Mary's tallest tower (right)

THE BASICS

✚ J4

✉ Kościół Mariacki, may be seen and heard anywhere in and around Rynek Główny

🕐 Hourly day and night, just after the clock chimes the hour. Tower visits: 3 May–Sep Tue, Thu, Sat 9–11.30, 1–5.30

♿ None

🎫 Free to listen in square; tower visits inexpensive, free on 1 May 12.10–3.30, and 2 May 9–11.30, 1–5.30

HIGHLIGHTS

● View of Barbican and St. Florian's Gate
● View in the opposite direction of Wawel Hill
● For a nominal sum the bugler will pose for a picture with you and give you his autograph and a stamp certifying that you climbed the tower

In a city of wonderful sights, it's strange that the most potent symbol is not seen but heard. The *hejnał*, or bugle call, has sounded from the top of the tallest tower of St. Mary's Church across Krakow's skyline for centuries, and continues to do so today, every hour, round the clock.

The legend The origin of the *hejnał* lies in an era when Krakow was under constant threat of Tatar invasion. One night in 1240, the sentry in St. Mary's Watchtower saw Tatar horsemen approaching just before dawn and sounded his bugle to rouse the troops and citizens. A Tatar arrow caught him in the throat, cutting short his bugle call. Though the sentry was killed, the citizenry had sufficient warning to fight off the invaders and save the city. The sentry was buried with great honor, and down the centuries his bugle call has continued to be played, with the final note cut short in his memory.

Climb the tower Today, the bugler is a member of the modern-day descendants of the watchmen, the fire brigade. In summer, you can climb the 239 steep steps to the little room 54m (177ft) above the ground, where, if you time it right (you won't be allowed to hang around indefinitely, as it gets very crowded up there), you can see the bugler in action. The *hejnał* has become a symbol of Poland and is relayed on Polish radio to mark the hour. If you can't climb the tower, do wave when you hear the *hejnał*—the bugler usually waves back.

Kamienice

You can see noblemen's town houses dating back more than 750 years throughout the Old Town but the market square is an ideal place to appreciate them—you don't even have to leave your café table to do so.

Location, location Krakow's Old Town was built following the Tatar invasions that devastated cities all over Poland. In 1257, a charter was granted and the city was laid out according to a regular plan whose streets and squares are still there today. Ownership was strictly defined and all residents, already a multicultural community owing to Krakow's position as a crossroads of European trade, were deemed equal under the rule of the local authorities.

Grand designs The houses—and especially the facades—have changed over the centuries, being remodeled after fires, and in line with fashion and their owners' fortunes. Gothic gave way to Renaissance and baroque style as Italian architects were called in to make them into palaces. One or two houses are now museums and many contain restaurants, shops or bars, so you can often wander in to see their beautiful details such as vaulted and decorated ceilings. The custom of marking each house with a sign above the door has persisted (*pod* means "under the sign of"). With competing modern shop signs and continuing renovations you are unlikely to spot all the signs on one tour, but keep looking and you'll collect a fair few.

THE BASICS

✚ H4
✉ Rynek Główny
☎ None
🕐 Daily 24 hours
🍴 Many and various (€–€€€)
♿ The square is cobbled but otherwise flat; few shops have ramps
🎟 Free

HIGHLIGHTS

● Restored ceilings in the restaurant at Kamienica Szara (No. 6)
● Gothic fighting lizards over the door at Kamienica Pod Jaszczurami (No. 8)
● Wierzynek restaurant in Kamienica Morsztynowska (No. 16)
● 18th-century Virgin painted on the facade of Kamienica Pod Obrazem (No. 19)
● The white eagle on Kamienica Pod Orłem (No. 45)

Kościół Mariacki

HIGHLIGHTS

● Veit Stoss's High Altar
● Slack Crucifix with a figure of Jesus carved from one piece of stone by Veit Stoss
● Silver altar of St. Joseph
● Biblical carvings on choir stalls
● 1890s murals by Jan Matejko
● Great West Window with stone tracery by Matejko, and stained glass by Mehoffer and Wyspiański

DID YOU KNOW?

● So lifelike is Veit Stoss's carving that in the 1930s a Krakow professor used it to study medieval skin diseases.
● It's said that Półzygmunt, one of St. Mary's five bells, was carried up the tower in 1438 by one man, Stanisław Ciołek.

If you see one church in Krakow it should be St. Mary's, a Gothic masterpiece: Its two mismatched towers built by rival brothers dominate the city skyline and its interior is crammed with world-class carvings.

City symbol From all over the city you can see St. Mary's two towers, the shorter bell tower topped with a baroque cupola, and the spire of the taller Watchtower encircled by a gold crown. The church entrance between these is for worshipers only; other vistors enter through a side door in Plac Mariacki.

Brick beauty St. Mary's basilica was built between the end of the 13th century and the beginning of the 15th, though the towers and side chapels were not finished until much later,

Clockwise from far left: The High Altar; the High Altar and stained-glass windows; the church's Gothic towers; the Jan Sobieski plaque; detail of the dying Virgin Mary on Veit Stoss's altar

and some of the additions made by artists of the Young Poland movement date from about a century ago. There are also several Renaissance tombs made by Italian artists.

High altar The rich colors and carving inside the basilica can make it difficult to pick out what to look at, but you should focus on the High Altar. Carved between 1477 and 1489 by the best sculptor of the day, Veit Stoss, known as the Master of Nuremburg, it is the largest altar of its kind in Europe. For his work, Veit Stoss was paid the equivalent of the city's budget for a whole year. In several folding sections, the oak and lime-wood altar, measuring 11m (36ft) by almost 13m (42ft), is adorned with around 200 gilded and painted figures, mostly relating to the life of the Virgin Mary—but the faces are people of Krakow who Stoss met in daily life.

THE BASICS

mariacki.com

✚ J4

✉ Plac Mariacki 5

☎ 12 422 5518

🕐 Mon–Sat 11.30–6 (the High Altar opens at 11.50), Sun 2–6; no visitors during Mass

🍴 None

♿ Few ramps

💰 Inexpensive

❓ Ticket office is opposite the side door on the other side of plac Mariacki

Pałac Krzysztofory

TOP 25

The Fontana Room (left); sculpture in the cellar (middle); the palace facade (right)

HIGHLIGHTS

● Fontana stucco ceilings
● Arcaded courtyard
● Exhibition on the history of Krakow
● Exhibition of Christmas cribs (*szopki*) in December from the first Thursday in the month

Is it a palace, a museum or a club? Built in the grand manner, the Krzysztofory Palace, home to a museum of Krakow's history and culture, has something for everyone, especially at Christmas.

Italian style Built on medieval foundations in the 17th century and named for Św. Krzysztof (St. Christopher), this grand house is arranged around an arcaded Tuscan courtyard; the second floor museum has fine stucco ceilings by Italian artist Baldassare Fontana. The great and the good have always stayed here, among them Stanisław August Poniatowski, the last king and duke of the Polish-Lithuanian Commonwealth. Later on, the palace was a hotbed of revolutionary fervor, housing members of the national government during the 1846 Krakow Uprising.

History and happenings Nowadays, the palace is the headquarters of the Historical Museum of the City of Krakow and the permanent exhibition is about the history and culture of the city. There are also changing temporary exhibitions. The cellars host the latest cutting-edge music and theater, while the Fontana Room holds regular classical concerts.

Christmas story In December, children and adults compete in making Christmas cribs, which go on show at the palace. Most of these *szopki* are in the traditional shapes of Krakow's best-loved buildings, but originality abounds.

Bar in the cellar (left); dining room (right)

Restauracja Wierzynek

When you begin with a banquet attended by almost half the crowned heads of Europe, as Mikołaj Wierzynek did in 1364, it's a hard act to follow, yet heads of state and celebrities are welcomed at this restaurant to this day.

Wedding feast Wierzynek's grand gesture—which he could well afford as a banker and mayor to the salt-rich district of Wieliczka—was to celebrate the marriage of the granddaughter of King Kazimierz the Great to Holy Roman Emperor Charles IV. The guests included the kings of Denmark, Hungary and Cyprus. Some say King Kazimierz had a diplomatic motive and wanted to ease growing political tensions in Europe. Whatever the reasons, a good time was had by all, and Wierzynek's gifts of silver plates to each guest went down well with the nobility. After the feast, the king granted Wierzynek a permit to entertain prominent visitors to the city, starting a tradition that continues today. Diners have included former American president George Bush Sr., former king of Spain Juan Carlos, and movie director Steven Spielberg.

Renaissance spirit The whole building has been expertly restored to Renaissance style, with splendid tiled stoves and coffered ceilings. Each of the restaurant's many rooms has a different theme, while the café has a lighter, more modern menu and decor; you can see Wierzynek's own well in the vaulted cellar bar. The main restaurant serves Old Polish cuisine.

THE BASICS

wierzynek.com.pl

H4

Rynek Główny 15

12 424 9600

Daily 1–11

Restaurant (€€€), café (€€) and cellar bar and grill (€)

Elevator

HIGHLIGHTS

● The Knights' Hall
● The visitors' book
● The view over the market square
● Princely service
● Wild boar, roe deer and roast sturgeon with Polish crayfish on the menu

TIP

● Though the café and cellar bar are more relaxed, reservations are recommended for the main restaurant.

Sukiennice

HIGHLIGHTS

● Renaissance and
Modernist gargoyles
● One-stop souvenir
shopping
● High-quality goods

DID YOU KNOW?

● The knife that the
jealous builder of St. Mary's
Watchtower used to kill his
brother, builder of the bell
tower, hangs on one of
the walls.

TIP

● Don't haggle—it's not
done in the Sukiennice. In
any case, you'll find prices
are no higher than in the
rest of Krakow and many
of the stalls, particularly
those selling jewelry, are
branches of shops else-
where in the city.

**In Krakow, even the main shopping
mall, the Cloth Hall, dates from the
13th century. Today's stallholders have
everything a souvenir hunter needs,
from leather bags to wooden dragons.**

Enterprise More than 100m (110 yards) long
and sitting proudly in the main square, Krakow's
old Cloth Hall emphasizes the central role of
trade in the development of the city. The original medieval building was developed under
Kazimierz the Great in the 14th century but,
after a fire in the mid-16th century, was rebuilt
in curvaceous Renaissance style with stone
masks along the parapets. As time went on
many other stalls and shacks were erected
around it, until a grand sweep of town planning

Clockwise from far left: A café in the arcades; a stall selling icons; the exterior of the Cloth Hall; shoppers in the entrance arcade; stained-glass decorations

THE BASICS

✚ H4

✉ Rynek Główny 1–3

☎ None

🕐 Souvenir stalls daily 10–8

🍴 Cafés in the arcades

♿ Few but flat access

💷 Free

Sukiennice Gallery

mnk.pl

✉ Sukiennice, Rynek Główny 3

☎ 12 433 5400

🕐 Tue–Sun 10–6

💷 Inexpensive

Rynek Underground

✉ Sukiennice, Rynek Główny 1

☎ 12 426 5060

🕐 Mon 10–8, Tue 10–4, Wed–Sun 10–10

💷 Moderate; free Tue

cleared them all away in the 19th century. The flower sellers in the square are the only outside traders who survived the clean-up.

Stalls The souvenirs on sale are good quality, mainly traditional Polish crafts: leather bags, sheepskins, small stained-glass angels, carved wooden figures, wooden boxes, jewelry, linen and embroidered folk costumes. Children may like the toy dragons and pint-sized chainmail.

Exhibitions The upper floor of the Cloth Hall is devoted to a gallery of 19th-century Polish art including about 450 paintings and many sculptures, while in the underground vaults an exhibition tells the story of the area in a series of interactive and imaginative displays.

More to See

DOROŻKI

dorozki.krakow.pl

Drawn up along the edge of the main square, Krakow's horse-drawn cabs add a tang to the atmosphere that even the nearby flower stalls can't mask. The horses are beautifully turned out with tassels and plumes. Look at their hooves: their shoes have a special rubber sole to protect their feet on the cobbled streets. Choose whichever one you like—no need to take the first in line.

➕ H3 ✉ Rynek Główny ☎ 12 431 2520 (Mon–Fri 10–5) 🕐 Daily from early morning until the small hours 🍴 Cafés nearby 💰 Expensive, the fixed price depends on the length of the journey: The shortest is around the main square, about 100PLN (€23); the longest a round-trip to Wawel and Kazimierz, about 300PLN (€70)

KAMIENICA HIPOLITÓW

mhk.pl

It's all very well looking at the palatial facades, but what was life like behind them? This museum demonstrates how wealthy families lived between the 17th and 19th centuries, though the house itself dates back to the 14th century.

➕ J3 ✉ plac Mariacki 3 ☎ 12 422 4219 🕐 May–Oct Wed–Sun 10–5.30; Nov–Apr Wed, Fri–Sun 9–4, Thu 12–7. Closed 2nd Sun of month all year 🍴 Magia café at entrance 💰 Inexpensive, free Wed

KOŚCIÓŁ ŚW. BARBARY

It's easy to overlook the modest entrance to St. Barbara's Church between the visitors' entrance to St. Mary's and the ticket office. Dating from the end of the 14th century, the church was supposedly built with the bricks left over from St. Mary's. Renovations are ongoing; the painted ceiling has already been restored to its former glory. Look, too, for the early 15th-century Pietà and a crucifix from the same century on the high altar.

➕ J4 ✉ Maly Rynek 8 ☎ None 🕐 Daily according to the times of services; German Mass Sun 7pm 🍴 Many cafés nearby 💰 Free

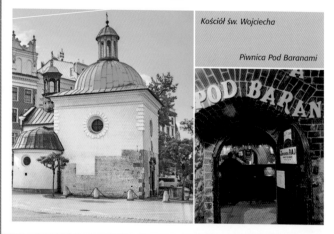

Kościół św. Wojciecha

Piwnica Pod Baranami

KOŚCIÓŁ ŚW. WOJCIECHA

This little gem of a baroque church built on Romanesque foundations is one of the oldest buildings in Krakow and still much used by locals. The best way to visit is to sit quietly in a rear pew—you'll see everything at a glance, including the image of the saint whose name is usually given as St. Adalbert in English. A small archaeology museum under the church has finds from the church and square.

🚩 H4 ⊠ Rynek Główny 3 ☎ 12 422 7100 ⏰ Museum Jun–Sep daily 10–4, but often closed if wet 🍴 Cafés in the square 🏷 Inexpensive

PIWNICA POD BARANAMI

piwnicapodbaranami.pl

On the corner of ul. św. Anny and the main square, the grand Dom Pod Baranami ("House under the Sign of the Rams") harbors Poland's most famous cabaret, founded by Piotr Skrzynecki (▷ 34) in 1956. The vaulted brick cellar (piwnica) still hosts cabaret, but mostly it is an alehouse where you can drink in the atmosphere along with the beer. The building also includes arts venues, including one of Krakow's best cinemas.

🚩 H4 ⊠ Dom Pod Baranami, Rynek Główny 27 ☎ 12 421 2500 ⏰ Cabaret night Sat 9pm–last customer; bar daily 11am–last customer 🍴 Café/bar 🏷 Inexpensive ❓ Book cabaret tickets in advance Mon–Fri 11–3 at 26 ul. św. Tomasza ☎ 12 421 2500

POMNIK ADAMA MICKIEWICZA

Not only was Adam Mickiewicz Poland's greatest Romantic poet, he was also an activist who gave voice to the vision of the restoration of the Polish nation, dying in exile in 1855 while forming a Polish legion to fight for his homeland. His statue is a favorite meeting place for Cracovians. If you find his name a mouthful, refer to him by his nickname, Adaś, as the locals do.

🚩 H4 ⊠ Rynek Główny between Sukiennice and Szara Restaurant 🍴 Many cafés in the square 🏷 Free

Horse-drawn carriages (dorożki) wait for customers in the square

Adam Mickiewicz statue

POMNIK PIOTRA SKRZYNECKIEGO

The statue of Piotr Skrzynecki, sitting in a convivial pose outside the Vis-à-Vis bar, stops many a visitor who may go on to "share" a drink with the jolly bronze without knowing who he is. Of course, Krakow is the kind of place where one very easily makes new friends in bars, and the anarchic Skrzynecki was an exceptional example of this trait. In 1956, he founded a landmark institution in Krakow's rich theatrical heritage—the cabaret at the Piwnica Pod Baranami (▷ 33), which continues next door to this day. Skrzynecki died in 1997 but the flower he usually carries shows how fresh and important his memory is.

➕ H4 ✉ Rynek Główny 29 🍴 Outside Vis-à-Vis bar 🎟 Free

WIEŻA RATUSZOWA

mhk.pl

The lions guarding the steps to Krakow's Town Hall tower must always have been as sleepy as they are today because the rest of the Town Hall, which had suffered many fires, ruins and rebuildings since 1316, was snatched away under their noses in 1820 during a general tidying-up of the main square. The tower itself, leaning badly by 1703, has been repaired, so you can try climbing to the top. Although the steep stone stairs are narrow and ascend to about the same height at St. Mary's, there are spacious former council chambers on the way up in which to rest. At the top there are good views on three sides—towards Wawel Hill, Kopiec Kościuszko and past St. Mary's Church to Nowa Huta— with inexpensive telescopes provided. Inside, you'll see the workings of the former and current (atomic) Town Hall clock.

➕ H4 ✉ Rynek Główny 1 ☎ 12 426 4334 🕐 Daily May–Oct 10.30–6. Closed in winter 🍴 Café and theater in cellar 🎟 Inexpensive, buy tickets from Tourist Information Office on ground floor. Inexpensive photo permits extra

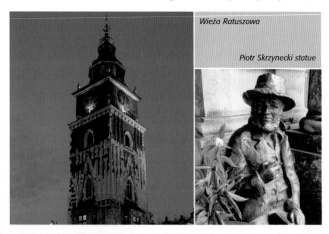

Wieża Ratuszowa

Piotr Skrzynecki statue

Around the Rynek Główny

This is where to take the pulse of the city. Listen out for the *hejnał* from St. Mary's Tower and look up to see the ornamental parapets.

DISTANCE: 800m (0.5 miles) **ALLOW:** 45 mins to 2 hours

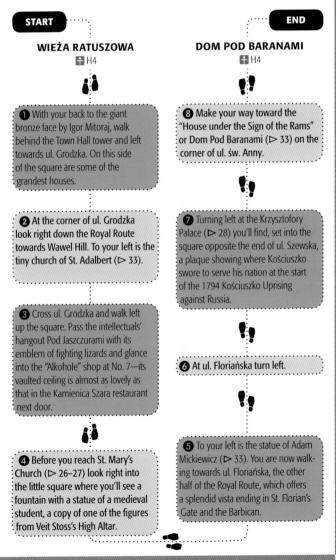

START

WIEŻA RATUSZOWA
H4

1 With your back to the giant bronze face by Igor Mitoraj, walk behind the Town Hall tower and left towards ul. Grodzka. On this side of the square are some of the grandest houses.

2 At the corner of ul. Grodzka look right down the Royal Route towards Wawel Hill. To your left is the tiny church of St. Adalbert (▷ 33).

3 Cross ul. Grodzka and walk left up the square. Pass the intellectuals' hangout Pod Jaszczurami with its emblem of fighting lizards and glance into the "Alkohole" shop at No. 7—its vaulted ceiling is almost as lovely as that in the Kamienica Szara restaurant next door.

4 Before you reach St. Mary's Church (▷ 26–27) look right into the little square where you'll see a fountain with a statue of a medieval student, a copy of one of the figures from Veit Stoss's High Altar.

END

DOM POD BARANAMI
H4

8 Make your way toward the "House under the Sign of the Rams" or Dom Pod Baranami (▷ 33) on the corner of ul. św. Anny.

7 Turning left at the Krzysztofory Palace (▷ 28) you'll find, set into the square opposite the end of ul. Szewska, a plaque showing where Kościuszko swore to serve his nation at the start of the 1794 Kościuszko Uprising against Russia.

6 At ul. Floriańska turn left.

5 To your left is the statue of Adam Mickiewicz (▷ 33). You are now walking towards ul. Floriańska, the other half of the Royal Route, which offers a splendid vista ending in St. Florian's Gate and the Barbican.

Shopping

ANTYKI SOSENKO
Upstairs in one of the tenement houses surrounding the Rynek is a spacious and atmospheric antique store, filled with furniture, paintings and many smaller objects and souvenirs from the past.
🔳 H3 ⊠ Rynek Główny 29 ☎ 12 423 2246 🕙 Mon–Fri 10–7, Sat 10–4

GALERIA PRZEDMIOTU AB
On the outer perimeter of the Cloth Hall, this gallery sells works by contemporary Polish artists and designers, including glass, ceramics and jewelry.
🔳 H4 ⊠ Sukiennice, Rynek Główny 1 ☎ 12 429 2340 🕙 Mon–Fri 11–7, Sat 11–5, Sun 12–4

KSIĘGARNIA KURANT
Kurant specializes in music scores, books and recordings. The large CD selection is particularly strong on classical music, featuring both traditional and contemporary composers.
🔳 H3 ⊠ Rynek Główny 36 ☎ 12 422 9859 🕙 Mon–Fri 9–7, Sat 10–4

PASAŻ 13
pasaz-13.pl
Aimed at business travelers, this petite, upscale shopping mall directly on Rynek Główny contains some of the top names of the retail world, as well as an aromatic deli selling food from across the globe, a couple of snazzy bars, a wine cellar and a pricey café. Staff generally speak English.
🔳 H4 ⊠ Rynek Główny 12–13 ☎ 12 617 0250 🕙 Mon–Sat 9–9, Sun 11–5

SUKIENNICE
If your time is limited, shop here for souvenirs and jewelry (▷ 30–31).
🔳 H3–4 ⊠ Rynek Główny 1–3 🕙 Daily 10–8

SZAMBELAN
szambelan.pl
A short distance from Rynek Główny, this tiny laboratory-like shop sells the famous Polish vodka flavored with various herbs, fruit and flowers, as well as a range of oils, jams and vinegars.
🔳 H4 ⊠ ul. Bracka 9 ☎ 12 628 7093 🕙 Mon–Thu 11–8, Fri–Sat 11–8.30, Sun 12–6

WAWEL
wawel-sklep.com.pl
This sweet shop is a Polish institution. Look for chocolate-covered plums, praline-centered Michałki and chestnut-flavored Kasztanki. Chocolates, sweets and biscuits are sold by weight and also in elegant presentation boxes, of which the most popular is the Królewski Smak (Royal Taste) selection.
🔳 H3 ⊠ Rynek Główny 33 ☎ 12 423 1247 🕙 Daily 10–7

ZEBRA
If sightseeing has been too hard on your feet, come here for a large selection of well-priced men's and women's shoes, both fashionable and practical.
🔳 H4 ⊠ Rynek Główny 7 ☎ 12 421 4034 🕙 Mon–Sat 10–8, Sun 10.30–6

FOREVER AMBER

Amber, or *bursztyn*, has been bought and sold here since Roman times, when the main trade routes ran from the Baltic to the Mediterranean and to Asia along the Silk Road. Baltic amber, the solidified resin of prehistoric pine trees, was found in Tutankhamun's tomb and was also used as an offering at the temple at Delphi. Don't buy for investment unless you are an expert, and remember it's not as tough as gemstones. An insect trapped in amber makes an unusual piece.

Entertainment and Nightlife

BONEROWSKI PALACE

pro-arts.pl

Weekly 90-minute Chopin recitals are performed in this noble mansion, now restored to former glory.

⊞ H3 ✉ ul. św. Jana 1 ☎ 12 374 1300
🕙 Sat 7pm

BORO

Relax on the leather sofas of this courtyard-level club in the Pod Baranami building—for coffee early on, and DJs and live music later.

⊞ H4 ✉ Rynek Główny 27 ☎ 693 922 010
🕙 Nightly 5pm–last customer

DOM POLONII

orfeusz.eu

This smart and central venue stages Chopin piano recitals (lasting about 80 minutes) by well-known performers. Concerts of Polish folk and Jewish music concerts, are also sometimes held here, mainly in summer.

⊞ H4 ✉ Rynek Główny 14 ☎ 662 007 255
🕙 Chopin concerts daily 6pm

HARRIS PIANO JAZZ BAR

harris.krakow.pl

This cellar bar often has more atmosphere than air. Live bands perform several times a week.

⊞ H4 ✉ Rynek Główny 28 ☎ 12 421 5741, reservations possible 🕙 Mon–Fri 1pm–last customer, Sat–Sun 11am–last customer

KRZYSZTOFORY PALACE

classica.krakow.pl

Come here for classical music played by the Cracow Philharmonic Quartet in the 17th-century Fontana Room upstairs. Meanwhile, the cellar hosts regular club nights with adventurous music tending towards electronica. In summer, clubbers spill out into the courtyard to chill.

⊞ H3 ✉ Rynek Główny 35; cellar club enter from ul. Szczepańska 2 ☎ Classical concerts: 501 638 750; cellar club: 12 422 2236 🕙 Classical concerts Sun 7pm; other classical music concerts usually Wed and Sat; nightly cellar club nights 5pm–last customer

THE PIANO ROUGE

thepianorouge.com

The red carpet down to this elegant air-conditioned cellar club, bar and restaurant sets the tone for live music—pop and blues as well as jazz.

⊞ H3 ✉ Rynek Główny 46 ☎ 12 431 0333
🕙 Sun–Thu 9pm–2am, Fri–Sat 9pm–4am

POD JASZCZURAMI

podjaszczurami.pl

The studenty bar "Under the Sign of the Lizards" has been buzzing since 1969. It has an ever-changing schedule that includes music, debates, lectures, movies and other events.

⊞ H4 ✉ Rynek Główny 8 ☎ 12 429 4538
🕙 Mon–Wed 10am–1am, disco nights Thu–Sat 10am–4am, Sun 11am–1am

SHOWTIME

Live bands play nightly among the crimson seats and zebra heads. A varied music policy tends toward pop and rock for over-21s.

⊞ H3 ✉ Rynek Główny 28 ☎ 12 421 4714
🕙 Sun–Thu 7pm–2am; Fri–Sat 7pm–4am

DRINK LOCAL

In winter, you can sample *miód pitny z goździkami* (hot mead with cloves), *grzaniec galicyjski z migdałami* (hot sweet wine with almonds) or *piwo grzane* (heated beer with sweet syrup); the syrup can be *imbirowym* (ginger), *malinowym* (raspberry) or *wiśniowym* (cherry). In summer, try the same *sok* (juice) flavors in your cold beer.

Where to Eat

<table>
<tr><td colspan="1">PRICES</td></tr>
</table>

PRICES

Prices are approximate, based on a
3-course meal for one person.
€€€ over 170PLN/€50
€€ 100–170PLN/€30–€50
€ under 100PLN/€30

EUROPEJSKA (€€)

europejska.pl

This smart café has a decor that harks
back to a more formal age, with gleam-
ing wood fittings and striped wallpaper.
It serves dishes from all over Europe.

➕ H3 ✉ Rynek Główny 35 ☎ 12 429 3493
🕙 Daily 8am–midnight

HAWEŁKA (€€€)

hawelka.pl

Founded by Antoni Hawełka in 1876,
this traditional restaurant serves Polish
classics in a smart room. There's an
even more upscale salon, Restaurant
Tetmajerowska, above, decorated with a
fresco by Włodzimierz Tetmajer.

➕ H3 ✉ Rynek Główny 34 ☎ 12 422 0631
🕙 Daily 11–11

KAWIARNIA RATUSZOWA (€)

The café in the basement of the Town
Hall tower spreads out into the main
square in summer—making it a great
choice for people-watching.

➕ H4 ✉ Rynek Główny 1 ☎ 12 421 1326
🕙 Daily 9am–midnight

RESTAURACJA SZARA (€€)

szara.pl

This is one of the most beautiful rooms
on the square, with a Belle Époque
ambience under a lofty vaulted ceiling.
The international menu with a Polish
accent features delicacies such as
smoked reindeer tartare and butter-fried
pike-perch.

➕ H4 ✉ Rynek Główny 6 ☎ 12 421 6669
🕙 Daily 11–11

WENTZL (€€€)

restauracjawentzl.com

This many-roomed restaurant has been
here since 1792 and its salons are
crammed with pictures of celebrated
diners. Chef Zbigniew Siemieniec's
Polish and French specialties include
beef tongue with black truffles.

➕ H4 ✉ Rynek Główny 19 ☎ 12 429 5299
🕙 Daily 12–11

WESELE (€€)

weselerestauracja.pl

Authentic Polish cooking done just the
way it should be is the star turn at this
two-level Rynek restaurant decorated in
romantically Polish fashion.

➕ H4 ✉ Rynek Główny 10 ☎ 12 307 8700
🕙 Daily 12–11

WIERZYNEK (€€€)

wierzynek.com.pl

The oldest restaurant in Krakow (▷ 29)
offers accomplished Polish cuisine and
expert service.

➕ H4 ✉ Rynek Główny 15 ☎ 12 424 9600
🕙 Daily 1–11

GAME ON

In contrast to the less expensive eating
places elsewhere in the Old Town, which
are heavy on dumplings and other carbs,
the premier restaurants in the Rynek
Główny highlight traditional ingredients
gathered from the wild. This is the place to
try boar, boletus mushrooms or pike-perch.
You might find a menu featuring grilled
saddle of fallow deer or a starter of *rydze*
(milk-cap mushrooms). Sophisticated
rather than rustic, the flavors are often
reminiscent of the best Italian cooking.

Within the Planty

Krakow's Old Town holds more than enough treasures to keep you busy for a week. Here you'll find university buildings, a fine art collection and dozens of medieval and baroque churches.

Top 25

Collegium Maius **42**

Jama Michalika **44**

Kamienica Szołayskich **45**

Kościół Franciszkanów **46**

Muzeum Książąt Czartoryskich **48**

Pałac Biskupa Erazma Ciołka **50**

More to See **51**

Walk **55**

Shopping **56**

Entertainment and Nightlife **57**

Where to Eat **58**

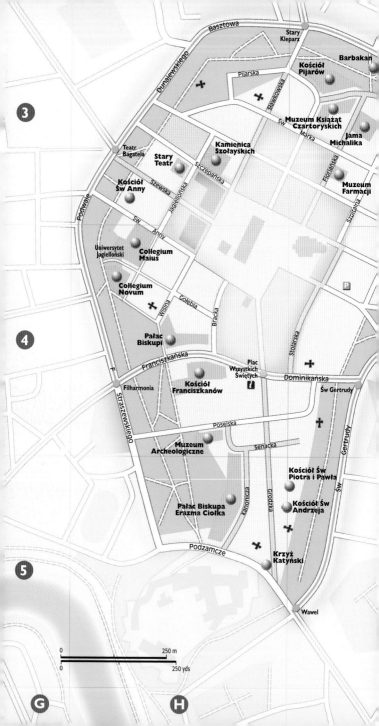

Collegium Maius

HIGHLIGHTS

- Musical clock
- Jagiellonian Globe of 1508, the first to show America
- Wooden carving of Kazimierz the Great from about 1380
- Astrolabe from Cordoba made in 1054
- 17th-century Persian carpets
- Rector's gold chain dating from AD500
- Polish director Andrzej Wajda's Oscar
- Mementoes of Moon landings

DID YOU KNOW?

- The figures on the courtyard clock were carved in the 1950s. The clock is computer controlled; it plays at 9am, 11am, 1pm, 3pm and 5pm.
- Visit the cellar coffee shop U Pęcherza (☎ 12 663 1518 ◷ Mon–Fri 7–5, Sat 8–5, Sun 9–5) and you'll be in the oldest part of the building.

The oldest university building in Poland, the Collegium Maius sums up the history of learning in this city of more than 40,000 students—and has some modern surprises in its museum.

Ancient lessons The Krakow Academy, which pre-dated the university, was founded in 1364 by Kazimierz the Great. It was revived here by Queen Jadwiga, who gave her crown jewels to fund it, and her husband King Władysław Jagiełło, who donated this building in 1400. There was a clock in the courtyard even then, but the musical clock that plays the university song, *Gaudeamus Igitur*, while university figures walk round the dial, is 20th-century.

Old studies Upstairs, beneath the traditionally painted ceiling of the library, you'll see portraits

Clockwise from far left: Heraldic frieze with the coat of arms of Cardinal Frederick Jagiellon, university chancellor in the 15th century, on the left; the courtyard; detail of a water feature; the figures of the musical clock

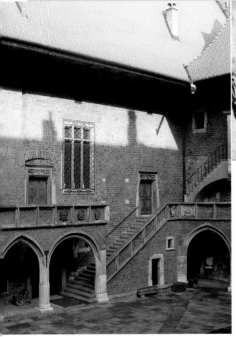

THE BASICS

uj.edu.pl/muzeum
maius.uj.edu.pl

H4

✉ ul. Jagiellońska 15

☎ 12 422 0549, 12 663 1307

🕐 Main exhibition 30-min tours Mon, Wed–Fri 10–2.20, Tue 10–3.20. Main exhibition plus scientific and fine arts collections, hour-long tour Mon–Fri only 1pm. World of the Senses Mon–Sat 9–1.30

🍴 Cellar café (€)

♿ Good

💰 Main exhibition: inexpensive, free Apr–Sep Tue 3–5.20; longer tour with scientific and fine arts collections: moderate; World of the Senses: inexpensive, Sat free

❓ Advance booking recommended, especially for tours in English: main Collegium Maius tours: tel 12 663 1521; World of the Senses: tel 12 663 1319

of the university's eminent scholars. Then come professors' rooms, complete with period furniture and an enormous variety of objects and treasures from the university's beginnings up to the present day. The Stuba Communis, or refectory, features a 14th-century sculpture of Kazimierz the Great; the Treasury has three 15th-century scepters and the only preserved drawing by Veit Stoss, creator of the altar in St. Mary's Church. A whole room is dedicated to the revolutionary astronomer Nicholas Copernicus, who studied here from 1491 to 1495. The portraits of some of the professors murdered by the Nazis in World War II are movingly displayed in the Jagiellonian Hall. After all the "look, don't touch" displays, children particularly may enjoy getting their hands on the separate interactive World of the Senses science exhibition.

Jama Michalika

Glass ceiling by Karol Frycz (left); the café's sumptuous interior (right)

TOP 25

THE BASICS

jamamichalika.pl

☩ J3

✉ ul. Floriańska 45

☎ 12 422 1561

🕐 Sun–Thu 9am–10pm, Fri, Sat 9am–11pm

💷 Inexpensive

♿ Main room is on ground floor

HIGHLIGHTS

● Green balloon still hanging from the ceiling
● Century-old marionettes from the popular satirical Christmas shows
● Art nouveau stained glass
● Cakes, especially *sernik* (cheesecake) and Wawel cake

While not the oldest such establishment in the city, this is the one that sums up what Krakow café society is all about. People, the arts and fashion have moved on, but this place showed them the way.

Cabaret set "Michalik's Den" was set up in 1895, and soon attracted the cream of the city's writers, artists and actors. Within a decade it had become the home of Zielony Balonik— the Green Balloon cabaret—which poked fun at the bourgeoisie of the day. At the same time, it became the unofficial headquarters and meeting place of the Młoda Polska, or Young Poland, movement. The art nouveau furniture and furnishings of the café are still much as they were in its heyday. The walls hung with paintings, puppets, caricatures and all manner of artwork reinforce the fin-de-siècle atmosphere. Of course, a green balloon takes pride of place.

Café chat Though now more frequented by older middle-class customers gossiping over cheesecake rather than wild bohemians, Jama Michalika is a good starting point from which to explore Krakow's café society. There are hundreds of cafés in the Old Town alone and they have nothing in common with the global chains that have taken over other European cities, or with each other. Most are small, many open late—often until the last guest leaves—and nearly all serve alcohol as well as coffee, snacks and homemade cake. Now, as ever, the patrons provide the entertainment.

Model of Wawel Hill as an Acropolis (left); Self Portrait with Wife, 1904 (middle); detail of a staircase (right)

Born in the city in 1869, the son of a sculptor, Stanisław Wyspiański left his mark everywhere in Krakow, as a painter, playwright, sculptor, designer and professor. All these strands are drawn together in the Szołayski House, a historic town house now part of the National Museum.

Star pupil Wyspiański began his short but creative life—he died of syphilis aged 38—by studying art history at the Jagiellonian University and painting at the Academy of Fine Arts. There he was taught by Jan Matejko, who soon engaged him to help renovate St. Mary's Church in the Rynek Główny. By 1890, the young artist had embarked on a tour of Europe, studying in Paris for three years, where he mingled with artists such as Gauguin and shared a studio with his compatriot Józef Mehoffer.

Home boy Returning to Krakow, Wyspiański plunged into city life, taking his home town and the Polish nation as his main themes. He seemed to work on everything: stained-glass windows; a costume for the Lajkonik folk figure that is still in use; portraits; posters; and plays, including one called *Wesele (The Wedding)*, censored at the time, which is now much admired. Through it all he was a moving spirit in the Young Poland movement, which paralleled the European Modernists. The museum also has a charming exhibition with mementoes of Wisława Szymborska—a poet from Krakow who won the Nobel Prize for Literature in 1996.

THE BASICS

mnk.pl

H3

plac Szczepański 9

12 292 8183,
12 422 7021

Tue–Sat 10–6, Sun 10–4

Café (€)

Few to temporary exhibitions on ground floor

Inexpensive; free Sun

HIGHLIGHTS

● Wyspiański's model of Wawel Hill as a Polish Acropolis
● *Planty with a View onto Wawel*, oil, 1894
● Bannisters and cartoon of a window showing *Apollo for the Medical House*
● Pastel portrait of Wyspiański's daughter, *Little Helena*
● Interior design for the apartment of Tadeusz "Boy" Żeleński, a doctor, translator and writer
● Last self-portrait, 1907

Kościół Franciszkanów

HIGHLIGHTS

● Gothic, Renaissance and baroque murals in the cloisters
● Mehoffer's 1933 Stations of the Cross
● Wyspiański's art nouveau window *God the Father—Become!*
● Wyspiański's flower-painted walls and ceilings
● Master Jerzy's 16th-century *Mater Dolorosa*

TIP

● You can see changes in the stained-glass windows as the light strikes them at different times of day.

After being almost destroyed in the great fire of 1850, the 13th-century Franciscan Church was redecorated early in the 20th century by the celebrated artists Stanisław Wyspiański and Józef Mehoffer.

New for old More than any other in Krakow, the Franciscan Church demonstrates how the city's artists, while remaining resolutely contemporary, engage with the history of the city to restore and enliven it. Built between 1237 and 1269 by Henry the Pious for the newly arrived Franciscan monks, this was one of the first brick churches in the city. Duke Władysław Jagiełło, husband of Queen Jadwiga, was baptized here in 1386. Damaged by Swedish invasions, the church was rebuilt again in baroque style, only to be destroyed, along with some of its

WITHIN THE PLANTY TOP 25

priceless artifacts, in the great fire of Krakow, and then rebuilt in a mixture of styles.

Art of glass Sit in the main body of the church to appreciate the beautiful stylized flowers and stars—reflecting the Franciscans' love of nature—painted on the walls and ceilings, the work of Wyspiański, who also created the stained-glass windows. But older treasures have survived. Look in the side chapels for the tomb of Giovanni Gemma, the Venetian court doctor who died in 1608, and the earlier Virgin Mary surrounded by angels. Outside, you'll find a modern artwork—seven stone and steel angels by Michał Batkiewicz, which appear to be praying toward the window across the street from which Pope John Paul II used to greet the faithful when he was Archbishop of Krakow.

THE BASICS

✚ H4
✉ plac Wszystkich Świętych 5
☎ 12 422 5376
🕐 Daily 6am–7.45pm
🚫 None
✋ Free

WITHIN THE PLANTY TOP 25

For more than two centuries the Czartoryski family have been amassing choice pieces of art, including a Leonardo da Vinci portrait of a beautiful young woman, *Lady with an Ermine*.

Patriotic princess With the idea of preserving Poland's heritage, Princess Izabela Czartoryska began collecting art and curiosities at her palace at Puławy in the late 18th century. Among the first items the heiress bought were Turkish trophies from the siege of Vienna a century before, and Polish royal treasures from Wawel. She was a romantic magpie and soon added Shakespeare's chair, bits of the grave of Romeo and Juliet, the ashes of El Cid and his wife, and relics of Abelard and Héloïse. By 1798, her son Prince Adam Jerzy, traveling in Italy, had

Clockwise from far left: The museum's exterior; an archway joins the museum buildings; Roman busts on display; the Czartoryski coat of arms

acquired Leonardo's *Lady with an Ermine* and Raphael's *Portrait of a Young Man*, which became the jewels of the collection. In 1876, the city of Krakow offered its old arsenal as a home for the collection, and the museum was born. It is currently undergoing renovation, with the new museum due to reopen in December 2019. In the meantime you can see *Lady with an Ermine* at the National Museum (▷ 90–91).

War torn In World War II, the best pieces were taken by the Nazis for Hitler's private collection, while the curator died in a concentration camp. Many of the items were later returned, though 844 are still missing, including the precious Raphael. An empty frame hangs in the museum awaiting its return.

THE BASICS

muzeum-czartoryskich.krakow.pl

czartoryski.org

✚ J3

✉ ul. św. Jana 19; entrance also at ul. Pijarska 8

☎ 12 422 5566

🕐 Currently closed for restoration

♿ None

🎟 Inexpensive, Sun free

TIP

● Remember that, as in all Krakow's museums, the last ticket is sold half an hour before closing. This rule is very strictly enforced here.

Pałac Biskupa Erazma Ciołka

TOP 25

The Ciolek coat of arms (left) on the striking pink facade of the Erazma Palace (right)

THE BASICS

muzeum.krakow.pl

☩ H5

✉ ul. Kanonicza 17

☎ 12 429 1558,
12 424 9370

🕐 Mon–Fri 10–4

♿ Very good, elevators and ramps to most sections

🎫 Art of Old Poland gallery inexpensive; Orthodox Art gallery inexpensive; combined ticket moderate

HIGHLIGHTS

● Madonna of Krużlowa, c. 1410

● *St. Hieronymus* by Hans Dürer (brother of Albrecht)

● Padovano angels of 1533

● 16th-century wooden statue of Christ riding a donkey

● Mandylion, imprint of Christ's face on a cloth

● Karol Wojtyła's rooms in Archdiocesan Museum

● Archdiocesan Museum's Małopolska Madonnas

As well as housing superb collections of sacred art, this restored palace in Krakow's oldest and best-preserved street has many original medieval and Renaissance details.

Carved beauty One of most beautiful houses in Krakow, Bishop Erazm Ciołek's Palace dates from the beginning of the 16th century. Today, his residence contains two exhibitions of religious art. The Art of Old Poland rooms begin with a small group of 12th-century stone carvings discovered in local churches and cloisters. There follows a collection of wooden Madonnas, saints and altars dating from the 14th to 16th centuries, also from churches in the region. One room is devoted to the work of Veit Stoss, the master carver of St. Mary's altar.

Sacred icons The second exhibition, of Orthodox art of the old Polish-Lithuanian Republic, comprises a priceless collection of 15th- and 16th-century Carpathian icons, plus later icons showing the Renaissance and baroque influence that came once the Orthodox Church had accepted Rome in 1596.

Pope's progress The Archdiocesan Museum next door has a large collection of sacred art and a reconstruction of the rooms of the future Pope John Paul II, who lived in the Deanery at No. 21 as a priest in the 1950s. The John Paul II Center stands opposite at No. 18.

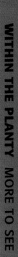

More to See

BARBAKAN

mhk.pl

This grand fortification protected the old Royal Route that led to Wawel Hill and also formed part of an important trade route. First raised at the end of the 15th century, today it stands like an isolated fort. Climb into the upper galleries for a good view over the city. In summer (Jun–Sep) there are regular medieval pageants and knightly combats inside.

J3 ☒ ul. Basztowa ☎ 12 422 9877 🕐 Mid-Apr to Oct daily 10.30–5 💰 Inexpensive (ticket also gives entry to the city walls and the Celestat Museum ▷ 94)

BRAMA FLORIAŃSKA

Florian's Gate is where future kings of Poland traditionally entered the city on their way to be crowned at Wawel Cathedral. Today you can visit the remaining city walls either side of the gate and read interesting explanations of how each city guild had its own defensive part to play. The haberdashers and

carpenters seem to have made a pretty good job of it, coached by the Marksmen's Guild.

J3

COLLEGIUM NOVUM

This grand, red-brick university administrative building was constructed in the 1880s on the site of the 15th-century Jerusalem and Philosophers' halls of residence. All the university's big ceremonies take place in its Aula Magna, or Great Hall, which is hung with magnificent paintings. You may see graduates in traditional robes having their photos taken outside, but your best chance of seeing the Aula is to attend a concert there.

H4 ☒ ul. Gołębia 24 🕐 Not open to tourists, view outside only from the Planty, unless attending a concert ♿ Planty access flat, ul. Gołębia cobbled

KOŚCIÓŁ ŚW. ANDRZEJA

Dating from the end of the 11th century, St. Andrew's is an unusual Romanesque survivor in a city

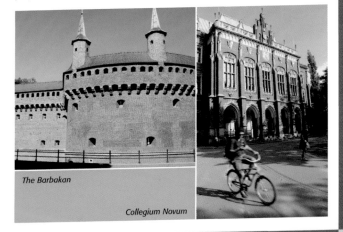

The Barbakan

Collegium Novum

remade in Gothic and later styles—perhaps because it was the only church in the city to escape the mass destruction of the Tatar invasion of 1241. Nonetheless, its two white towers are topped with baroque cupolas, and inside you'll find baroque stucco by Baldassare Fontana and an ebony and silver tabernacle.

➕ J5 ✉ ul. Grodzka 56 🕐 Daily 7.30–5 🍴 Café nearby 💷 Free

KOŚCIÓŁ ŚW. ANNY

A high point of baroque in Krakow, the university church of St. Anne's was built at the end of the 17th century. Once your eyes have taken in the dazzling gilded and painted cupola and the pulpit held aloft by gold angels, you will be drawn to the main altar, sculpted by Baldassare Fontana and dedicated to św. Jan Kęnty, a professor and saint buried here in 1473.

➕ H3 ✉ ul. św. Anny 11 ☎ 12 422 5318 🕐 Daily 7am–9pm 🍴 Cafés nearby ♿ None 💷 Free

KOŚCIÓŁ PIJARÓW

Rising ornately at the end of ul. św. Jana, the rococo facade of the Piarist Church was added by Francesco Placidi about 30 years after the church was built at the beginning of the 18th century. The restored interior features magnificent *trompe-l'oeil* paintings by Franz Eckstein; the atmospheric crypt is often used for concerts.

➕ J3 ✉ ul. Pijarska 2 🕐 Daily 7–7

KOŚCIÓŁ ŚW. PIOTRA I PAWŁA

Consecrated in 1635 and the first completely baroque church in Poland, SS. Peter and Paul is easy to recognize from the line of statues of the apostles separating it from ul. Grodzka. Inside, you'll find fine baroque stuccowork, tombs and an organ loft. There's also a model of Foucault's Pendulum, which demonstrates the rotation of the Earth. Jesuit preacher Piotr Skarga, whose statue dominates Plac św. Marii Magdaleny opposite, is buried in the crypt.

Kościół św. Anny

Dome of Sw. Piotra i Pawła

➕ J5 ✉ ul. Grodzka 54 🕐 Daily 7–7, later for concerts; demonstration of Foucault's Pendulum Thu 10, 11, 12

KRZYŻ KATYŃSKI

At the end of ul. Grodzka, outside the 14th-century Kościół św. Idziego (St. Giles Church), a simple wooden cross commemorates the massacre of some 22,000 Polish officers by Russian troops in the forest of Katyń in March 1940. The victims included many academics, doctors and lawyers, as Stalin aimed to eliminate Poland's intelligentsia.
➕ H5 ✉ ul. św. Idziego 1

MUZEUM ARCHEOLOGICZNE

ma.krakow.pl

See Egyptian mummies and other ancient artifacts here. Highlights include finds from the local Małopolska region, including Światowid, an early pagan idol resembling a stone totem pole.
➕ H4 ✉ ul. Senacka 3; enter garden and museum from ul. Poselska 3 ☎ 12 422 7100, 12 422 7560 🕐 Jul–Aug Mon–Fri 11–6, Sun 10–3; Sep–Jun Mon, Wed, Fri 9–3, Tue, Thu 9–6, Sun 11–4 💰 Inexpensive; permanent exhibition free Sun; English audio guide inexpensive; garden inexpensive

MUZEUM FARMACJI

muzeumfarmacji.pl

The Pharmacy Museum is a fascinating collection celebrating the apothecary's art. The 22,000 exhibits, including pills, potions and instruments, are displayed over several floors of a lovely building dating from the 15th century. Under the Renaissance ceilings, pickled snakes and strange herbs share shelves with jars of leeches, while the basement houses an alchemist's laboratory complete with dried bats and crocodiles. It's said that Faust studied at the Jagiellonian University, though whether Krakow is where he sold his soul to the devil is not known.
➕ J3 ✉ ul. Floriańska 25 ☎ 12 422 4284 🕐 Tue 12–6.30, Wed–Sun 12–2.30 💰 Inexpensive

Muzeum Archeologiczne

Bottles inside the Muzeum Farmacji

PAŁAC BISKUPI

The bishops of Krakow have lived on this site since the 14th century, but today this 17th-century building opposite the Franciscan Church attracts special reverence as the 1963–1978 residence of the former Archbishop of Krakow, Karol Wojtyła, who later became Pope John Paul II. He conducted his celebrated conversations with the young people of Krakow and blessed the faithful from the "Pope's Window" over the main doorway.

➕ H4 ✉ ul. Franciszkańska 3

POMNIK KOPERNIKA

The statue of Copernicus near the Collegium Novum represents the great astronomer as a young man. Copernicus studied astronomy at the Krakow Academy from 1491 to 1495, though he did not publish his revolutionary theory that the Earth orbits the sun until 1543.

➕ H4 ✉ ul. Gołębia/Planty

STARY TEATR

stary.pl

Created in the late 18th century from several older buildings, the Old Theater was restored to its 1905 art nouveau splendor after World War II, which had left it in ruins. Inside, the ceilings are painted with flowers and the walls are lined with portraits and busts of the greatest names in Polish theater. Some plays are staged with English surtitles (check schedule).

➕ H3 ✉ ul. Jagiellońska 5 ☎ 12 422 4040 🎦 Museum Tue–Sat 11–1 and from an hour before curtain-up

TEATR IM JULIUSZA SŁOWACKIEGO

slowacki.krakow.pl

Built in the 1890s, the Słowacki Theater, which can seat 900, is a great wedding-cake of a building, modeled on the Paris Opera by Jan Zawiejski and encrusted with detail.

➕ J3 ✉ plac św. Ducha 1 ☎ 12 424 4525 🎦 Box office Mon 10–2, 2.30–6, Tue–Sat 9–2, 2.30–7, Sun 3–7 🍴 Café (€)

The Słowacki Theater

Statue of Copernicus at the Collegium Novum

A Stroll around the Planty

In the 1800s, Krakow's crumbling city walls were replaced by a leafy green ring of gardens shaded by trees and ideal for strolling.

DISTANCE: 4km (2.5 miles) **ALLOW:** 1.5–2.5 hours

START

PLAC WSZYSTKICH ŚWIĘTYCH
🚌 H4 🚋 Tram to ul. Dominikańska

END

RYNEK GŁÓWNY
🚌 H4 🚋 Tram to ul. Dominikańska

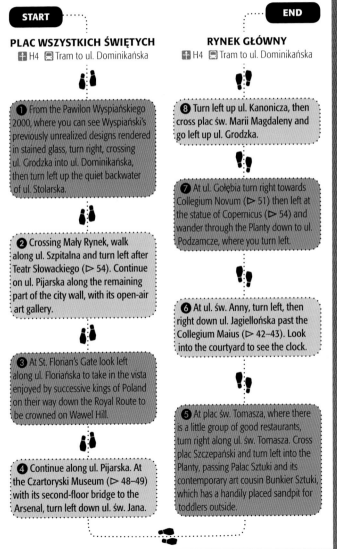

① From the Pawilon Wyspiańskiego 2000, where you can see Wyspiański's previously unrealized designs rendered in stained glass, turn right, crossing ul. Grodzka into ul. Dominikańska, then turn left up the quiet backwater of ul. Stolarska.

② Crossing Mały Rynek, walk along ul. Szpitalna and turn left after Teatr Słowackiego (▷ 54). Continue on ul. Pijarska along the remaining part of the city wall, with its open-air art gallery.

③ At St. Florian's Gate look left along ul. Floriańska to take in the vista enjoyed by successive kings of Poland on their way down the Royal Route to be crowned on Wawel Hill.

④ Continue along ul. Pijarska. At the Czartoryski Museum (▷ 48–49) with its second-floor bridge to the Arsenal, turn left down ul. św. Jana.

⑧ Turn left up ul. Kanonicza, then cross plac św. Marii Magdaleny and go left up ul. Grodzka.

⑦ At ul. Gołębia turn right towards Collegium Novum (▷ 51) then left at the statue of Copernicus (▷ 54) and wander through the Planty down to ul. Podzamcze, where you turn left.

⑥ At ul. św. Anny, turn left, then right down ul. Jagiellońska past the Collegium Maius (▷ 42–43). Look into the courtyard to see the clock.

⑤ At plac św. Tomasza, where there is a little group of good restaurants, turn right along ul. św. Tomasza. Cross plac Szczepański and turn left into the Planty, passing Pałac Sztuki and its contemporary art cousin Bunkier Sztuki, which has a handily placed sandpit for toddlers outside.

Shopping

CLICK

clickfashion.pl

One in a small chain of Polish fashion boutiques, Click sells reasonably priced women's clothes and accessories. The classic styles are strong on color and good for all ages.

⊞ H4 ✉ ul. Grodzka 32 ☎ 12 422 4281
🕐 Mon–Sat 11–8, Sun 12–7

CRACOW POSTER GALLERY

cracowpostergallery.com

This is the only gallery in the country specializing in Polish promotional and commercial posters. It stocks more than 2,000 vintage film and exhibition posters by about 100 Polish artists.

⊞ J4 ✉ ul. Stolarska 8–10 ☎ 12 421 2640
🕐 Mon–Fri 11–7, Sat 11–5

DEKOR ART

This eye-pleasing store is crammed to the gills with colorful Polish ceramics from Bolesławiec, bearing simple but beautiful folk designs.

⊞ H3 ✉ ul. Sławkowska ☎ 515 452 969
🕐 Mon–Sat 10–6

DIAMENT

diament-jubiler.pl

There's silver and amber of course at this jeweler's, but Andrzej Skibiński is also a master goldsmith and will make jewelry to order.

⊞ H4 ✉ ul. Grodzka 62 ☎ 12 422 8707
🕐 Mon–Fri 10–7, Sat–Sun 10–5

GALERIA ORA

galeria-ora.com

Come here for a tempting selection of high-quality modern jewelry by local designers who work in silver, amber and a variety of more unusual gemstones.

⊞ H4 ✉ ul. św. Anny 3/1a ☎ 781 661 212
🕐 Mon–Sat 10–8, Sun 11–6

GALERIA OSOBLIWOŚCI ESTE

You may not be allowed to take the rhinoceros skull out of the country, but there are plenty of other fascinating things new and old from all over the world in this cabinet of curiosities.

⊞ H3 ✉ ul. Sławkowska 16 ☎ 12 429 1984
🕐 Mon–Fri 11–7, Sat 11–3

KARMELLO

karmello.pl

Karmello produces high-quality Polish pralines in a range of interesting flavors. You can also sample their products on the spot, accompanied by coffee or drinking chocolate.

⊞ J3 ✉ ul. Floriańska 40 ☎ 535 002 475
🕐 Mon 7am–10pm, Tue–Sun 7am–11pm

KRAKOWSKI KREDENS

krakowskikredens.pl

This classy food store, devoted to fine local produce, all beautifully packaged, sells biscuits, cakes, preserves, cheeses and more. The cold meat counter is a tribute to Polish ingenuity.

⊞ H4 ✉ ul. Grodzka 7 ☎ 12 423 8159
🕐 Mon–Fri 10–7, Sat 11–7, Sun 11–5

POLSKIE SZKŁO

This shop sells a large selection of traditional and modern Polish glass and crystal, as well as Christmas decorations all year round.

⊞ H4 ✉ ul. Grodzka 36 ☎ 12 422 5739
🕐 Mon–Fri 10–7, Sat 10–3

ART AND CRAFT

Robiony ręcznie, meaning "handmade," is a phrase you'll come across a lot in Krakow, especially within the Old Town, where most of the ornaments, glass, jewelry, stained glass, toys and carvings are created by local artisans. The quality is usually high.

Entertainment and Nightlife

CAFÉ PHILO

A very friendly crowd squeeze into this small bar to chat and debate, making it a good place to meet new people.
🔖 J3 ✉ ul. św. Tomasza 30 🕐 Daily 10am–last guest

CLASSICAL MUSIC

There are so many classical music performances in the Old Town that it's difficult to escape the promotional leaflets. Try to catch an hour-long concert in a church or historic building. Tickets are usually sold on the door. Timings will vary according to season but here is a typical selection:

Chopin 🔖 H3 ✉ Pod Gruszką Journalists' Club, ul. Szczepańska 1; Teatru Słowackiego; Pałac Bonerowski 🕿 604 093 570 🕐 Most nights of the week 7pm

Concerts in churches
Kościół św. Piotra i Pawła 🔖 H5 ✉ ul. Grodzka 54 🕿 695 574 526 🕐 Most nights of the week. Organ concerts 5pm, chamber music 8pm
Kościół O. O. Bernadynów 🔖 H5 ✉ ul. Bernardyńska 2 🕿 695 574 526 🕐 Tue, Sat 8.30pm
Kościół św. Idziego 🔖 H5 ✉ ul. Grodzka 67 🕿 695 574 526 🕐 At least 2 nights a week

CRACOW CINEMA CENTER ARS

ars.pl
On the site of Kino Sztuka, this is one of Poland's oldest cinemas. Several screens show original-language, mainly art-house, films with Polish subtitles.
🔖 H3 ✉ ul. św. Jana 6 🕿 12 421 4199; reservations dokina.pl 🕐 Daily various times

ENTERTAIN THE DRAGON

stawowy.pl
This annual summer season dinner show brings the Krakow cabaret tradition alive for English-speakers.
🔖 H3 ✉ Centrum Sztuki Moliere, ul. Szewska 4 🕿 602 772 265 🕐 Jul–Aug Fri 7pm

FILHARMONIA

filharmonia.krakow.pl
One of Poland's largest philharmonic auditoriums hosts a symphony orchestra, mixed choir and boys' choir. They specialize in large vocal and instrumental works and also play in Wawel Castle and the Collegium Novum.
🔖 H4 ✉ Filharmonia im. Karola Szymanowskiego w Krakowie, ul. Zwierzyniecka 1 🕿 12 422 9477, ext. 33, 12 429 1438, ext. 33 🕐 Ticket office Tue–Fri 10–2, 3–7, Sat–Sun 1 hour before the performance 🔵 Free admission for the blind, people with impaired mobility and their companions

JAZZ ROCK CAFÉ

jazzrockcafe.pl
People fall into this cellar and never want to leave, intoxicated by the electric atmosphere, wild dancing and loud rock music.
🔖 H3 ✉ ul. Sławkowska 12 🕿 514 909 907 🕐 Daily 7pm–6am

OPERA KRAKOWSKA

opera.krakow.pl
Krakow's opera performs a repertoire of Polish and European classics, in modern premises near the train station.
🔖 J3 ✉ ul. Lubicz 48 🕿 12 296 6200 🕐 Regular opera seasons, check with ticket office for performance schedule and times

PROZAK

This trendy basement club delivers fresh beats from both local and international DJs to a glitzy crowd over three packed dance floors.
🔖 H4 ✉ plac Dominikański 6 🕿 733 704 650 🕐 Fri–Sat 10pm–8am, Sun–Thu 10pm–6am

Where to Eat

WITHIN THE PLANTY | WHERE TO EAT

PRICES
Prices are approximate, based on a 3-course meal for one person. €€€ over 170PLN/€50 €€ 100–170PLN/€30–€50 € under 100PLN/€30

BAR MLECZNY POD TEMIDĄ (€)

bar-mleczny.com.pl

By far the best of the many inexpensive dumpling and pancake places in town, this old-fashioned "milk bar" (no alcohol) serves a wide variety of hot, tasty and very fresh Polish food fast.

➕ H4 ✉ ul. Grodzka 43 ☎ 12 422 0874 🕐 Daily 9–8

CAFÉ CAMELOT (€)

Sample light meals, good salads and Camelot's celebrated apple cake, all within 13th-century stone walls.

➕ H3 ✉ ul. św. Tomasza 17 ☎ 12 421 0123 🕐 Daily 9am–midnight

CECHOWA (€)

This old-fashioned Polish restaurant has customers who have been coming for decades. They serve excellent steak tartare and beef roulade with buckwheat.

➕ H3 ✉ ul. Jagiellońska 11 ☎ 12 421 0936 🕐 Daily 11–10

CHIMERA SALAD BAR (€)

This self-service restaurant with hot dishes and a salad bar has become a Krakow institution. At lunchtime, you may have to wait in line.

➕ H3 ✉ ul. św. Anny 3 ☎ 12 292 1212 🕐 Noon–last guest

COPERNICUS (€€€)

copernicus.hotel.com.pl

If you are inclined to splurge on haute cuisine, this is the place to do it. Go for the chef's tasting menu and a wine from the impressive selection.

➕ H5 ✉ Hotel Copernicus, ul. Kanonicza 16 ☎ 12 424 3400 🕐 Daily 12–11

CORSE (€€)

corserestaurant.pl

This Corsican restaurant has enjoyed an excellent reputation since it opened 20 years ago. The menu features a great selection of Mediterranean food.

➕ J4 ✉ ul. Poselska 24 ☎ 12 421 6273 🕐 Daily 1–11

GRUSZKA NOVA (€€)

gruszkanova.pl

This elegant, antique-filled restaurant serves a menu of well-executed Polish favorites under heavy chandeliers.

➕ H3 ✉ ul. Szczepańska 1 ☎ 534 174 506 🕐 Sun–Thu 12–10, Fri–Sat 12–12

KAWALERIA (€)

kawaleria.com

The Polish cooking here is accompanied by friendly and well-polished service. The lunch menu is available until 4pm.

➕ H4 ✉ ul. Gołębia 4 ☎ 12 430 2432 🕐 Daily 12–10

PETITE FRANCE (€)

petitefrancekrakow.pl

If you are tired of Polish food, head for this authentic French bistro for *escargots* or *camembert au pommes*.

➕ J3 ✉ ul. Szpitalna 20 ☎ 12 422 7513 🕐 Daily 9am–11pm

TABLE TALK
Smacznego!: bon appetit! *rezerwacja stolików*: table reservations *samoobsługa*: self-service *prosimy o zwrot naczyń*: please bring back your empty dishes

Wawel Hill

As the seat of bishops and kings, the limestone outcrop of Wawel Hill was the center of Church and State in Poland from the 11th century until the capital was moved to Warsaw in the late 16th century. The cathedral is still the resting place of Poland's heroes.

Top 25

Katedra Wawelska **62**

Pałac Królewski na Wawelu **64**

Smocza Jama **66**

More to See **67**

Where to Eat **68**

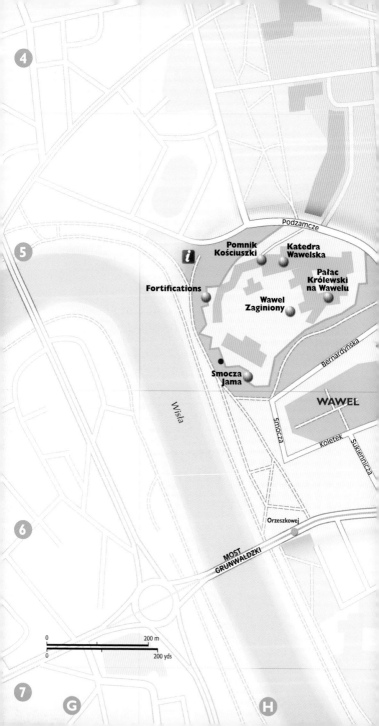

Wawel

Stradomska

ŚW
Agnieszki

J. DIETLA

Stradom

J

Katedra Wawelska

HIGHLIGHTS

● St. Stanisław's silver tomb

● Queen Jadwiga's leather and wood orb and scepter

● King Kazimierz the Great's Gothic tomb

● Mehoffer's stained-glass windows from the turn of the 19th/20th centuries

● Zygmunt chapel

● Zygmunt tower and bell

● Altar in the crypt where Karol Wojtyła, later to be the first Polish pope, said his first Mass

As well as being Poland's premier church, Wawel Cathedral has a bell that grants lovers' wishes, heroes in its crypt, the huge silver tomb of Poland's patron saint and the bones of ancient monsters hanging in its doorway.

Bishop's move Krakow's bishops took up residence on Wawel Hill from 1000, and work started on the first cathedral a couple of decades later; a second cathedral was begun in 1085 and consecrated in 1142. Of this, the Romanesque St. Leonard's crypt and a few stones survive. The three-aisle Gothic cathedral we see today was started in 1320 and consecrated in 1364. Most of the chapels, whose domes are so striking as you approach from the gardens, particularly the gold dome of the Renaissance Zygmunt chapel, were added later.

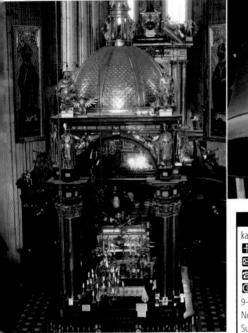

WAWEL HILL TOP 25

Coronation place The murdered St. Stanisław, former Bishop of Krakow, became a focus for unifying Poland, and his tomb in the cathedral a place of pilgrimage. The kings of Poland chose to be crowned next to his relics and to be buried here, too. The first was Władysław Łokietek ("the Short," called by Poles "the Elbow-high"). Walking around the church, you will see their stone and marble memorials, including that of Queen Jadwiga; their remains are mostly in the crypt.

Poets and politicians In another part of the crypt are the tombs of the great Polish Romantic poets, Adam Mickiewicz and Juliusz Słowacki. You'll also find the country's heroes: Tadeusz Kościuszko, Marshal Józef Piłsudski and General Władysław Sikorski, head of the Polish Government in Exile during World War II.

THE BASICS

katedra-wawelska.pl

H5

Wawel 3

12 429 3327

Apr–Oct Mon–Sat 9–5, Sun 12.30–5; Nov–Mar Mon–Sat 9–4, Sun 12.30–4; museum Mon–Sat 9–5. Closed holy days and national hols. Last admission an hour before closing

Cafés on Wawel Hill (€)

Few; lift from Bernardyńska Gate (steep cobbled road accessible by taxi) to garden level and toilets

Inexpensive

TIP

● If you touch the clapper of the Zygmunt bell with your left hand, they say you will be lucky in love.

Pałac Królewski na Wawelu

Wawel Castle is perhaps Poland's greatest treasure, despite the loss off some of its finest pieces to invaders. Many of these items have been tracked down and returned, and it's all been gleamingly restored—even the furniture polish smells good.

State power The kings of Poland began to live on Wawel Hill from the mid-10th century. King Alexander and his successor, Zygmunt the Old, commissioned a new palace in the Italian Renaissance style early in the 16th century, its arcaded courtyard decorated with frescoes that visitors can still see today. The last Jagiellonian, Zygmunt II Augustus, added a splendid collection of Brussels tapestries for the Royal Private Apartments, and by the end of the 16th century

Clockwise from far left: Inner courtyard; view of the castle from the river; two of the castle's towers; Coat of Arms Gate; frescoes on the walls of the Renaissance-style courtyard

THE BASICS

wawel.krakow.pl

➕ H5

✉ Wawel 5

☎ 12 422 5155, ext 219

🕐 All tickets are timed. State Rooms: Apr–Oct Tue–Fri 9.30–5, Sat–Sun 10–5; Nov–Mar Tue–Sat 9.30–4, Sun 10–4. Royal Private Apartments: Apr–Oct Tue–Fri 9.30–5, Sat–Sun 10–5; Nov–Mar Tue–Sat 9.30–4. Crown Treasury and Armory: Apr–Oct Mon 9.30–1, Tue–Fri 9.30–5, Sat–Sun 10–5; Nov–Mar Tue–Sat 9.30–4. Sun hours apply 1, 3 May, 15 Aug

🍴 Cafés on Wawel Hill (€)

♿ Few

💰 State Rooms: moderate, free Nov–Mar Sun. Royal Private Apartments: moderate. Crown Treasury and Armory: moderate, free tickets on the day Nov–Mar Mon

❓ There are two ticket offices at Bernardyńska Gate and Herbowa (Coat of Arms Gate). Last admission 1 hour before closing. The arcaded courtyard closes 30 min before the gates to Wawel Hill, which are open from 6am to dusk

Wawel Castle was one of the great cultural centers of Europe. In 1939, the tapestries and the gold coronation sword were taken to safety in Canada before the Nazis occupied the castle; they are back on display today.

Present riches The State Rooms were designed to impress, and still do—it's difficult to drag your eyes away from the carved and painted ceilings. The 30 heads that remain of the original 194 on the ceiling of the Deputies' Hall are so lifelike that you expect them to speak—apart from the one that is gagged, allegedly for telling the king what to do. To see the Royal Private Apartments and the choice paintings from the schools of Titian, Raphael and Botticelli you must join a tour; don't miss the Oriental Art exhibit.

Smocza Jama

TOP 25

Children examine dragon souvenirs (left); Bronisław Chromy's statue (right)

WAWEL HILL TOP 25

THE BASICS

wawel.krakow.pl

✚ H5

✉ Wawel Hill

☎ 12 422 5155,
12 422 6121

🕐 Cave: Jul–Aug daily
10–7; May–Jun daily 10–6;
Apr, Sep–Oct daily 10–5

🍴 Cafés on Wawel
Hill (€)

♿ None for cave, dragon
accessible from coach park
along level river path

🎟 Inexpensive, under-
7s free

HIGHLIGHTS

● Bronisław Chromy's
statue
● The dragon breathes
real flames
● Many fissured limestone
caverns

TIP

● You don't have to buy a
ticket for Wawel Castle or
the cathedral to visit the
Dragon's Lair. Just buy a
separate ticket from the
machine at the top of the
stairs down into the cavern.

The Smok, or dragon, is the popular symbol of Krakow, and emblem of the fire in the belly of this otherwise intellectual city. You will find its image everywhere, from green fluffy toys to jewelry and trade names.

The legend Long ago in the days when people first settled in this bend of the Vistula River, King Krak built his castle on Wawel Hill, little realizing that underneath him in one of the limestone caverns there slumbered a dragon. As the peasants took to grazing their sheep and cattle on the riverbanks, the dragon awoke and began seizing their livestock, sometimes carrying off young women too. The town was terrified and the king offered his daughter's hand in marriage and his whole kingdom to whoever could slay the beast. Knight after knight died fighting the creature, until a young shoemaker offered to try. He asked for sheepskins, mutton fat and a great deal of sulfur. By dawn he had constructed a fleecy ram, smeared with fat and stuffed with sulfur. The dragon woke and gobbled up the baited breakfast. As the sulfurous fire raged in its stomach, it drank and drank from the river to try to put it out—until eventually it exploded. The cobbler won the princess and the kingdom.

Today You can see the dragon, a spiky statue by Bronisław Chromy, by following the riverbank below Wawel Hill, or by climbing down 135 steps from the top of the hill, emerging at the river through the Dragon's Lair. The ferocious beast still emits a fearsome flame.

More to See

FORTIFICATIONS

Looking towards Wawel Hill from the Old Town, you will see many towers, but not all are defensive. The farthest away, from an Old Town vantage point, are the Clock, Zygmunt and Silver Bells towers of the cathedral. Seen from the east, the mainly Renaissance castle retains the Gothic Jordanka, Danish and Kurza Stopka (Hen's Foot) towers and the baroque Zygmunt III corner tower. Farther around the hill, toward the river, you'll find three tall brick towers, begun in the 15th century: Baszta Złodzieska or the Thieves' Tower; Baszta Sandomierska; and the Senators' Tower or Lubranka.

➕ H5 ✉ Wawel Hill ☎ 12 422 5155
🚫 None

POMNIK KOŚCIUSZKI

If you approach Wawel Hill from ul. Kanoniczka, the mounted statue of the soldier and engineer Tadeusz Kościuszko, designed by Leonard Marconi in 1921, can be seen near the Coat of Arms Gate. A Polish freedom fighter, Kościuszko also joined the Americans in their battle for independence and befriended Washington and Jefferson. In 1794, he declared the insurrection against the Russians in Krakow (later known as the Kościuszko Uprising).

➕ H5 ✉ Wawel Hill ☎ 12 422 5155
🍴 Cafés below the hill 🚫 None

WAWEL ZAGINIONY

The Lost Wawel exhibition is an atmospheric and imaginative collection based on the remnants of the Renaissance royal kitchens, what's left of the Gothic royal castle and a 9th-century chapel. It also includes archaeological finds from centuries of excavation. There are diagrams of the different phases of building on Wawel Hill, as well as computer simulations of the more important vanished buildings and a model of the hill in the 18th century.

➕ H5 ✉ Wawel 5 ☎ 12 422 5155, ext 219 🕐 Apr–Oct Mon 9.30–1, Tue–Fri 9.30–5, Sat–Sun 10–5; Nov–Mar Tue–Sat 9.30–4, Sun 10–4 🚫 None 💰 Inexpensive, free on the day Mon Apr–Oct; Sun Nov–Mar

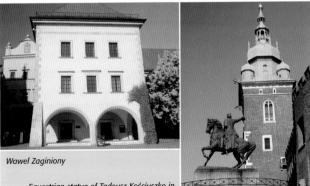

Wawel Zaginiony

Equestrian statue of Tadeusz Kościuszko in front of the castle

WAWEL HILL MORE TO SEE

Where to Eat

AQUARIUS (€)

aquariuskrakow.pl

Board the barge via a 7m-long (23ft)
gangplank for a choice of dining experiences. The formal restaurant downstairs
specializes in fish and seafood, while
the self-service café on the upper deck
offers an international menu.

➕ H5 ✉ Moored by Bulwar Czerwieński
(near Jubilat Department Store) ☎ 12 427
2003 🕐 Daily 12–10

KAWIARNIA POD BASZTĄ (€)

The Café Under the Tower is perfectly
sited for the weary tourist. Right on the
hill, it provides a full international menu
as well as drinks and snacks. In the
summer months, outside tables mean
you can eat your ice cream while looking across the gardens at some of
Krakow's most beautiful sights.

➕ H5 ✉ 9 Wawel ☎ 12 422 7528 🕐 Apr–
Jun, Sep–Oct Mon–Fri 9–5, Sat–Sun 9–6;
Nov–Mar daily 9–4; Jul–Aug daily 9–8 ♿ Lift
from Bernardyńska Gate (steep cobbled road
accessible by taxi) and toilets

POD BARANEM (€€)

podbaranem.com

One of the best restaurants in Krakow,
Pod Baranem serves quality versions
of traditional Polish dishes, including
excellent fish and venison options, in
a setting reminiscent of an elegant
bourgeois home.

➕ H6 ✉ 19 ul. św. Gertrudy 21 ☎ 12 429
4022 🕐 Daily 12–10

POD SMOCZĄ JAMĄ (€)

jama.krakow.pl

The dragon painted on the wall is trying
to quench the fire with beer, but most
of the diners choose from the traditional
Polish dishes or wide-ranging international fare on offer.

➕ H5 ✉ 24 ul. Podzamcze ☎ 12 422 2921
🕐 Mon–Sat 9–8, Sun 10–8

POD WAWELEM (€)

With its beerhall atmosphere, oompah
bands, wood-paneled dining room with
long benches and liter steins of lager,
this place feels like it's come straight
from Bavaria. The menu is mostly
Polish, though it also offers other Central
European dishes to soak up the beer.

➕ H6 ✉ ul. św. Gertrudy 26–29 ☎ 12 421
2336 🕐 Mon–Sat 12–12, Sun 12–11

SMAK UKRAIŃSKI (€)

ukrainska.pl

Experience the little-known cuisine of
Poland's neighbor at this delightfully
cozy cellar restaurant. The stone walls
are bedecked with traditional Ukrainian
embroidery and carpets from the
Carpathian Mountains, and the menu
includes lots of hearty Slavic comfort
food such as borsht, Kiev meatballs and
beef goulash with buckwheat.

➕ H5 ✉ ul. Kanonicza 15 ☎ 12 421 9294
🕐 Daily 12–10

GO GRILLING

All over Krakow, but particularly near the
river, you'll find informal open-air eating
places where you can barbecue your own
food. They are a good choice for a basic
lunch or dinner, usually washed down with
beer. Recognize them by the rustic wood
decor—tables might be old cable reels and
seats tree trunks still clad in bark.

Kazimierz

Founded by Kazimierz the Great in 1335, and incorporated into Krakow proper in 1791, Kazimierz today is full of new enterprise. It buzzes with bohemian clubs, shops and cafés, yet at the same time celebrates its rich Jewish history.

Top 25

Muzeum Etnograficzne **72**

Plac Nowy **74**

Stara Synagoga **75**

Synagoga i Cmentarz Remuh **76**

Żydowskie Muzeum Galicja **77**

More to See **78**

Walk **81**

Shopping **82**

Entertainment and Nightlife **83**

Where to Eat **84**

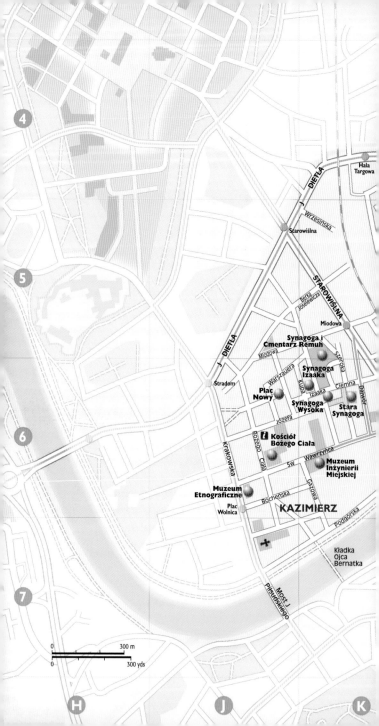

4

5

6

7

Hala Targowa

DIETLA

Wrzesińska

Starowiślna

STAROWIŚLNA

Berta Joselewicza

Miodowa

Miodowa

J DIETLA

Stradom

Synagoga i Cmentarz Remuh

Szeroka

Warszauera

Kupa

Synagoga Izaaka

Izaaka

Ciemna

Dajwór

Plac Nowy

Synagoga Wysoka

Józefa

Stara Synagoga

Kościół Bożego Ciała

Bożego Ciała

Św.

Wawrzyńca

Muzeum Inżynierii Miejskiej

Krakowska

Ciżowa

Muzeum Etnograficzne

Bocheńska

Plac Wolnica

KAZIMIERZ

Podgórska

Kładka Ojca Bernatka

Most J. Piłsudskiego

0   300 m
0   300 yds

H   **J**   **K**

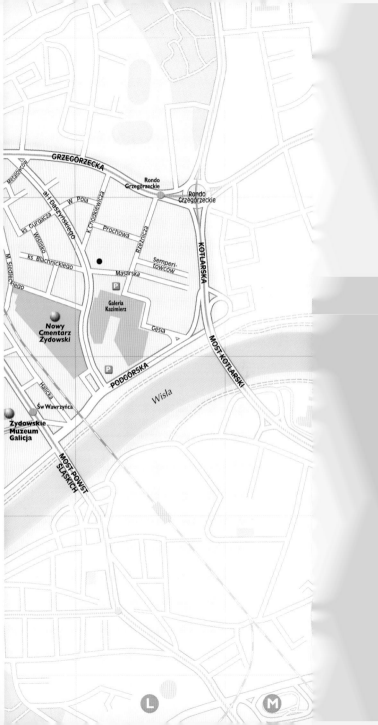

Muzeum Etnograficzne

HIGHLIGHTS

● Potter's workshop
● Krakowianka costumes
● Traditional Krakow Christmas cribs
● Display showing traditional festivals in the region

DID YOU KNOW?

● The bronze bas-relief on the northern wall showing Kazimierz the Great admitting the Jews to Poland is a version by Henryk Hochman of his 1910 original.

This museum devoted to the traditional life and customs of local people, particularly those in the surrounding countryside, has inhabited the old town hall of Kazimierz for almost 60 years.

Historic location The earliest mention of a town hall in plac Wolnica, the large market square of Kazimierz, was in 1369. The building you see today was built in the 16th century with later additions. It became redundant when Kazimierz was absorbed into Krakow in 1791 and ceased to be a separate town. The Ethnographic Museum moved here just after World War II.

Country lives Drawing its exhibits mainly from the 19th century, and initially the work of one

Clockwise from far left: Model of a traditional Polish country house; interior of a cottage from southern Poland; a colorful Christmas crib; traditional Polish costumes; window of a model house; museum exterior

amateur collector, Seweryn Udziela, the museum's collection of 80,000 items provides a fascinating glimpse of rural life and customs in Poland as they were until very recently. The interiors of the traditional cottages reconstructed in the museum show how everything, from the baby's crib to the butter churn, was handmade out of the most readily available material—wood. Many of the walls are painted with flower motifs, echoing the colorful embroidery on the folk costumes on display from various regions of Poland. You can compare how custom and habits differed between Małopolska, the region surrounding Krakow, and other parts of Poland. Don't miss the work of folk artists Nikifor Wawryluk and Józef Janos. The museum also has occasional special exhibitions devoted to other parts of the world.

THE BASICS

etnomuzeum.eu

✚ J6

✉ Ratusz, plac Wolnica 1

☎ 12 430 5575

🕐 Tue–Wed, Fri–Sat 11–7, Thu 11–9, Sun 11–3.

🚌 504 to Plac Wolnica. Tram 6, 8, 10, 13 to plac Wolnica

♿ Good, lift and ramp

💵 Inexpensive; special exhibitions also inexpensive

Plac Nowy

Alchemia bar on plac Nowy (left); antiques for sale (right)

THE BASICS

✚ J6

✉ plac Nowy

🕐 Stalls daily 8–4

🍴 Fast food daily 9am–2am (€)

🚋 Tram 3, 9, 19 to ul. Miodowa

♿ Flat but very uneven

HIGHLIGHTS

● A drink in Alchemia (▷ 83)

● A *zapiekanka* (half a baguette pizza-style with toppings) or plate of *placki* (potato pancakes) from Endzior in the green rotunda

● Sunday morning flea market

TIP

● As with any big city market, do watch out for pickpockets.

DID YOU KNOW?

● Plac Nowy is the focus of Krakow's popular Soup Festival each May.

As the center of bohemian Krakow, this is where people come to begin long hedonistic nights, but once it was known as "Jewish Square" and was the hub of a very different kind of life and trade.

Yesterday Something of the old days still lingers in plac Nowy, particularly in the daytime; there's a sense in which it has not fully joined 21st-century Kazimierz. Running along one side of the square, ul. Estery is said to be named for Esther, Kazimierz the Great's Jewish mistress, while nearby ul. Ciemna, or Dark Street, is so named because it had no street lighting until after 1900. This was always the trading square of a district that for a long time was cut off from Krakow by Stara Wiślna, the Old Vistula river, which was only filled in to form ul. Dietla in the late 19th century.

Today The Okrąglak, the green-painted round building in the center of the square, dating from about 1900 and once used as a kosher slaughterhouse, is occupied by vendors of Polish fast food. Their establishments are patronized by local workers and budget travelers, who stand at metal counters to eat, and each has its devotees. Alchemia, the bar and music hall that epitomizes bohemian Kazimierz, stands on one corner, and many other bars and clubs catering for the young and hip have opened in the area. More traditional restaurants with *klezmer* music are found along ul. Szeroka, which caters to tourists.

Stara Synagoga

The oldest surviving synagogue in Poland, this imposing Renaissance building at the top of Kazimierz's main square is now a museum and a good first stop for finding out about the area's Jewish history.

Florentine accent A synagogue was first erected here in 1407, partly built into the Kazimierz city walls. Today's structure was largely the work of Florentine architect Matteo Gucci in 1570, though he kept the form of the older brick-ribbed vaulting. Later in the 16th and 17th centuries, two women's prayer sections were added, as were other extensions to enable it to serve as both a religious and an administrative center for the Jewish community. In World War II, the chandeliers were taken by the Nazi governor, Hans Frank, and the building used as a warehouse. By the end of 1944, the vaulting had collapsed. It remained in a ruined state until the end of the 1950s, when renovation began to turn it into a museum.

Heritage restored In the wall at the main entrance you'll see a baroque alms box, while inside the main prayer hall the *bimah*, with a wrought-iron canopy over a 12-sided stone base, is a replica of the 16th-century original. The exhibition in the main hall is dedicated to objects related to the important holidays of the Jewish calendar, such as porcelain and silver plates for the Passover bread and *kiddush* cups used on the Sabbath. The most important is a scroll with the text of the Torah.

THE BASICS

mhk.pl
* K6
* ul. Szeroka 24
* 12 422 0962
* Apr–Oct Mon 10–2, Tue–Sun 9–5; Nov–Mar Mon 10–2, Tue, Thu, Sat–Sun 9–4, Fri 10–5
* Tram 3, 9, 19 to ul. Miodowa
* None
* Inexpensive, Mon free; English audio guide inexpensive

HIGHLIGHTS

* Menorah
* Late-Renaissance stone Ark
* Collection of drawings and paintings of the streets of old Kazimierz
* Original collecting box for alms
* Reconstructed *bimah* (Torah reader's platform)

Synagoga i Cmentarz Remuh

The Wailing Wall (left); detail of the bimah (middle); gravestones in the cemetery (right)

HIGHLIGHTS

● Plaque marking
the place where Moses
Isserles prayed
● 17th-century *bimah* door
● Late Renaissance Ark
with inscriptions carved
in 1558
● Renaissance collec-
tion box

TIP

● Women should cover
their shoulders and men
their heads. No visitors are
allowed during services.

DID YOU KNOW?

● Traditionally, no one
ever sits in the place where
Moses Isserles prayed. It is
marked by a burning lamp.

Second in age to the Old Synagogue, the Remuh Synagogue is the only one in Krakow where religious services are still held regularly. Despite its small size, it has an important place in Jewish culture.

Holy giant Founded in 1553 by Israel Isserles Auerbach, King Zygmunt August's banker, the synagogue is named after his son, the Talmudic scholar Rabbi Moses Isserles, whose name was shortened to Remuh. Jewish people from all over Europe settled in Kazimierz, bringing different customs with them. The Talmudic Academy, founded by Moses Isserles in 1550, was instrumental in unifying Judaic law for these disparate traditions.

Ancient tombs The rabbi is buried in the cemetery immediately behind the synagogue with the inscription "Between Moses and Moses, nobody arose in Israel to equal Moses." The cemetery, which was closed to burials in 1800, contains some of the oldest tombstones in Poland. When it was restored after the Nazi desecration of World War II, a row of shallowly buried tombstones was discovered. These have been erected to separate the cemetery from ul. Szeroka and are known as the "Wailing Wall."

Continuing tradition The synagogue was used for storage during the Nazi occupation and its treasures plundered. Today, it has been reno-vated in a simple fashion and is now run by the Jewish community.

Żydowskie Muzeum Galicja

The museum's book-store (left); attractively laid-out exhibition space (right)

Set up by the late British photographer Chris Schwarz, the Galicia Jewish Museum aims to shed new light on the history of Jewish Galicia, celebrating eight centuries of Jewish culture in Poland, while also commemorating those who perished in the Holocaust.

Vanished lives Chris Schwarz was already a successful photographer in London when he moved to Krakow to set up this museum in 2004. An inspired and inspiring figure, he regretted the way that the atrocity of the Holocaust had blotted out memories of the rich Jewish heritage in Poland and set about remedying that. On display here you'll find a permanent exhibition called Traces of Memory, consisting of photographs taken by Schwarz and a commentary by social anthropologist Professor Jonathan Webber. The two spent 12 years traveling together, documenting the Jewish past in Poland. The result is a completely original body of work.

New vision As well as an extensive bookshop, the museum has a rich program of events, many in English, in which visitors are welcome to take part. Its main brief is to commission exhibitions and publications about Jewish history and culture and run educational programs, while stimulating interfaith discussion and debate. The net is spread very wide. There might be a film showing in the evening, or perhaps a lecture or a *klezmer* concert.

THE BASICS

galiciajewish
museum.org

✚ K6

✉ ul. Dajwór 18

☎ 12 421 6842

🕐 Daily 10–6

🍴 Café (€)

🚃 Tram 1, 3, 9, 11, 12, 19 to ul. Starowiślna/ul. św. Wawrzyńca

♿ Excellent

💵 Inexpensive

❓ Many special events and temporary exhibitions. Contact the museum for details

HIGHLIGHTS

● Traces of Memory exhibition
● Bookshop
● *Klezmer* concerts—tickets at moderate prices

KAZIMIERZ TOP 25

More to See

KOŚCIÓŁ BOŻEGO CIAŁA

When Kazimierz the Great founded the new town, it needed a parish church, so Bożego Ciała (Corpus Christi) church was begun in 1342. First it was built in brick and wood, then, but gradually became greater and grander. By the end of the 16th century, it was a huge Gothic basilica, while the rich baroque interior, complete with golden pulpit and altar, was added in the 17th and 18th centuries.

➕ J6 ✉ ul. Bożego Ciała 26 ☎ 12 430 6290; 12 430 6294 🕐 Daily, services 6.30am–7pm 🚊 Tram 6, 8, 10, 13 to plac Wolnica 🎟 Free

MUZEUM INŻYNIERII MIEJSKIEJ

mimk.com.pl

If your taste runs to old machinery rather than old churches, the Museum of Urban Engineering might appeal. There's a permanent exhibition of old motorbikes and cars, mainly Polish-made, as well as a collection of public transportation

vehicles from decades gone by. For children aged five to nine, there's an interactive scientific area with lots of ropes and switches to push and pull, where many but not all the explanations are in English. It's housed in the former Krakow tram depot and bus garage.

➕ K6 ✉ ul. św. Wawrzyńca 15 ☎ 12 421 1242 🕐 Jun–Sep Tue, Thu, Sun 10–6, Wed, Fri–Sat 10–4; Oct–May Tue–Sun 10–4 🍴 Brasserie café/restaurant 🚊 Tram 6, 8, 10, 13 to plac Wolnica 🎟 Inexpensive

NOWY CMENTARZ ŻYDOWSKI

The New Jewish Cemetery opened in 1800 when the Remuh cemetery no longer had space. It is the resting place of many eminent Jewish people of Krakow, from rabbis to painters, professors and politicians. Just inside the entrance there is a memorial to those who died in the Holocaust.

➕ K5 ✉ ul. Miodowa 55 🕐 Sun–Fri 8–6. Closed Jewish holidays 🚊 Tram 3, 9, 19, 24 to ul. Miodowa 🎟 Free ❓ Men must cover their heads to enter

Corpus Christi Church

Tombstones in the New Jewish Cemetery

SYNAGOGA IZAAKA

According to legend, the largest of Kazimierz's synagogues was built in 1644, after its founder, Izaak Jakubowicz, found treasure. Tuscan columns supporting the women's gallery are indicative of its early baroque style. The stuccoed cradle vault is the largest in Krakow and there are still traces of 17th- and 18th-century wall paintings. After wartime desecration, the relatively recent renovation continues.

🏛 K6 ✉ ul. Kupa 18 ☎ 12 430 5577 🕐 Sun–Fri 9–7 🚋 Tram 3, 9, 19, 24 to ul. Miodowa 💰 Inexpensive

SYNAGOGA TEMPEL

krakow.jewish.org.pl

This was built in the 1860s as a progressive synagogue. Inside, you'll find a riot of well-restored stained glass, gilt and ornament with Sephardic influences, in contrast to the white walls of older synagogues in the area.

🏛 J5 ✉ ul. Miodowa 23–24 ☎ 12 429 5411 🕐 Sun–Fri 10–6. Closed Jewish holidays 🚋 Tram 3, 9, 19, 24 to ul. Miodowa 💰 Inexpensive ❓ Female visitors should cover shoulders, men their heads

SYNAGOGA WYSOKA

krakow.jewish.org.pl

The late 16th-century High Synagogue was so named because the prayer hall is on the second floor—originally there were shops below. In design, it has much in common with Prague's High Synagogue, underlining the close ties between the two cities in that period. Today it has a large, well-stocked bookshop.

🏛 K6 ✉ ul. Józefa 38 🚋 Tram 3, 9, 19, 24 to ul. Miodowa 💰 Inexpensive

ULICA SZEROKA

Ul. Szeroka is what remains of the main square of the old village of Bawjół, said to be the first site of the Krakow Academy, the forerunner of the Jagiellonian University.

🏛 K5 ✉ ul. Szeroka 🍴 Many restaurants and cafés 🚋 Tram 3, 9, 19, 24 to ul. Miodowa

Bookshop in Synagoga Wysoka

Café on ul. Szeroka

Jewish Heritage Trail

Winding back and forth through the streets of Kazimierz between the Jewish landmarks, you'll see how the area is changing fast.

DISTANCE: 3.5km (2 miles) **ALLOW:** 2–3 hours

START

STARA SYNAGOGA
🔲 K6 🚋 Tram 3, 13, 24 to ul. Miodowa

❶ Walking down ul. Szeroka, Remuh Synagogue (▷ 76) and the cemetery's "Wailing Wall" are on your left. Roughly opposite is the Popper Synagogue, now a youth center. At the end on the right, Klezmer-Hois is where the ritual baths once stood.

❷ Take the path by Klezmer-Hois, turn right down ul. Miodowa, cross ul. Starowiślna (watch out for the trams), and go straight on under the railway bridge to the New Jewish Cemetery (▷ 78) on your left.

❸ Retrace your steps, turning left on to ul. Starowiślna, cross it, and make your way down ul. Dajwór on your right. Here you'll find the Galicia Jewish Museum (▷ 77).

❹ At the end of the road turn right on to ul. św. Wawrzyńca. The Museum of Urban Engineering (▷ 78) is halfway down on your left.

END

PLAC WOLNICA
🔲 J6 🚋 Tram 6, 8, to ul. Krakowska

❾ Leaving the church, turn right down ul. św. Wawrzyńca towards Plac Wolnica. Here you'll find the Ethnographic Museum (▷ 72–73).

❽ Continuing down ul. Miodowa away from the Kupa Synagogue, turn left down ul. Bożego Ciała to the huge basilica for which it is named (▷ 78).

❼ Walk back to the corner of ul. Miodowa and ul. Podbrzezie to the Tempel Synagogue (▷ 79, pictured left).

❻ Continue to the top of ul. Kupa. The 1640s Kupa Synagogue is on your right.

❺ Cross back up ul. Wąska to ul. Józefa, where you'll find the High Synagogue (▷ 79). Turn right up ul. Kupa to the Izaak Synagogue (▷ 79).

Shopping

AUSTERIA

austeria.pl

Krakow's largest Jewish bookstore is in Synagoga Poppera—it's the best place to find books on the region's Jewish past.

⊞ K6 ⊠ ul. Szeroka 16 ☎ 12 422 2586
🕐 Sun–Thu 10–7, Fri–Sat 10–8

BLAZKO KINDERY

blazko.pl

It calls itself a jewelry art gallery and does not overstate the case, selling good-quality pieces from contemporary designers, mainly in acrylic and silver.

⊞ J6 ⊠ ul. Józefa 11 ☎ 508 646 298
🕐 Mon–Fri 11–6, Sat–Sun 11–5

GALERIA KAZIMIERZ

galeriakazimierz.pl

This air-conditioned mall has 130 shops, restaurants and cafés.

⊞ L5 ⊠ ul. Podgórska 34, near Most Kotlarski
☎ 12 433 0101 🕐 Daily 10–10

GALERIA SZALOM

There's nothing hard-edged in this contemporary art gallery, which offers quirky paintings and sculptures.

⊞ J6 ⊠ ul. Józefa 16 ☎ 12 290 3270
🕐 Mon–Fri 11–6, Sat 11–3

GALERIE D'ART NAÏF

If your appetite for this kind of art has been whetted in the Sukiennice, this gallery is where you'll find the real thing. The owner, Leszek Macak, is one of Poland's greatest specialists in the field.

⊞ J6 ⊠ ul. Józefa 11 ☎ 12 421 0637
🕐 Mon–Fri 11–5, Sat–Sun 11–3

LU'LUA

lulua.pl

This luxurious perfumery has a carefully edited selection of more than 20 exclusive world brands, among them Trumper's cologne for men and Annick Goutal for the ladies.

⊞ J6 ⊠ ul. Józefa 22 ☎ 12 430 0275
🕐 Mon–Fri 11–7, Sat 11–6

MAPAYA

mapaya.pl

In her small boutique, Polish designer Martyna Wilde sells beautiful, ethical clothes and accessories that are hand-made around the world.

⊞ J6 ⊠ ul. Józefa 3 ☎ 48 501 351 444
🕐 Mon–Sat 11–6

PRODUKTY BENEDYKTYŃSKIE

Just across from plac Wolnica, this is the place to buy goods produced by Benedictine monks—cheese, meat, honey, tea, juice and wine.

⊞ J6 ⊠ ul. Krakowska 29 ☎ 12 422 0216
🕐 Mon–Fri 9–6, Sat 9–2

SZPEJE

This antique—or rather, vintage—store has reasonably priced antiques, mostly from Poland's communist era (1950s to 1980s).

⊞ J6 ⊠ ul. Józefa 9 ☎ 48 733 200 074
🕐 Mon–12–6, Sun 10–5

BUDGET BUYS

Plac Nowy's market is excellent value. The food outlets in the green rotunda dish up huge plates of Polish staples for tiny prices—Endzior is the most celebrated. Choose a *zapiekanka*—half a long baguette with hot, pizza-type topping—or a portion of *placki* (potato pancakes), which would feed a family. There are fruit and vegetable stalls daily, as well as antiques and general junk on Saturdays and clothing on Sundays. There's also a Sunday morning flea market at plac pod Halą Targową in the nearby district of Grzegórzki.

Entertainment and Nightlife

ALCHEMIA

alchemia.com.pl

The freewheeling bohemian ambience and guttering candles here sum up the best of Kazimierz nightlife. Who else would schedule a "Peculiar Music Night"? Reservations are recommended for concerts, movies and gigs in the Music Hall.

🔼 J6 ✉ ul. Estery 5 ☎ 12 421 2200
🕐 Daily 9am–4/5am

JUDAICA FOUNDATION

judaica.pl

It's not all klubbing and *klezmer* in Kazimierz. At the Center for Jewish Culture you'll find debates, literary events and regular concerts of classical music and jazz.

🔼 J6 ✉ ul. Meiselsa 17 ☎ 12 430 6449
🕐 Changing program, see leaflets or website for details

KLUB PIĘKNY PIES

The latest incarnation of this long-established, itinerant club is a large Kazimierz joint attracting ex-pats, budget travelers, local artists and pub philosophers. Indie and rock dominate the playlist.

🔼 J6 ✉ ul. Bożego Ciała 🕐 Sun–Thu 4pm–3am, Fri–Sat 4pm–5am

KOLEKTKTYW DAJWÓR

This club, café and booze complex in a Kazimierz courtyard has several venues satisfying a range of musical tastes. Parties go on long into the early hours here and things can get a bit wild.

🔼 K6 ✉ ul. Dajwór 16 🕐 Daily 1pm–7am

MŁYNEK CAFÉ

On the edge of the Kazimierz nightlife vortex, this much recommended vegetarian café-bar hosts a program of poetry readings and art shows.

🔼 J6 ✉ plac Wolnica 7 ☎ 12 430 6202
🕐 Mon–Fri 9–8, Sat 9–4, Sun 2–8

PTASZYL

This cozy restaurant-bar is hung with lots to interest the eye, including the little fantastical birds that give it its name. The ambience is friendly and arty.

🔼 K6 ✉ ul. Szeroka 10 ☎ 509 987 102
🕐 Daily 8.30am–last guest

PUB PROPAGANDA

pubpropaganda.pl

Communist knickknacks and portraits of Lenin make up the ironic decor in this cult club.

🔼 K5 ✉ ul. Miodowa 20 ☎ 12 292 0402, 600 331 922 🕐 Daily 12pm–last guest

SINGER

The lace-and-old-sewing-machine decor that characterizes Kazimierz originated at Singer. The quirky bar is a popular place to while away a lazy day or evening.

🔼 J6 ✉ ul. Estery 20/ul. Izaaka 1 ☎ 12 292 0622 🕐 Daily 9am–last guest

STAJNIA

pubstajnia.pl

This friendly bar and Italian trattoria is popular with both visitors and locals. In summer, this is one of the most popular outdoor garden cafés in town.

🔼 J6 ✉ ul. Izaaka 7/1 ☎ 12 423 7202
🕐 Daily 9am–midnight

KLEZMER MUSIC

Klezmer is enjoying a revival. No one can resist the infectious tunes and the wonderful musicianship of those who play this traditional Jewish music. If it's new to you, pick one of the places that offers a *klezmer* band with the evening meal.

Where to Eat

PRICES

Prices are approximate, based on a 3-course meal for one person.
€€€ over 170PLN/€50
€€ 100–170PLN/€30–€50
€ under 100PLN/€30

AWIW (€)

awiw.pl

This Jewish pub-restaurant serves tasty Polish and Jewish dishes in an intimate vaulted dining room.

➕ K6 ✉ ul. Szeroka 13 ☎ 519 075 540
🕐 Daily 10–10 🚋 Tram to ul. Miodowa

GOŚCINIEC POD ZAMKIEM (€)

gosciniec.krakow.pl

Try the wild boar steaks or duck in this friendly place, which has free cabaret some evenings in the *piwnica* (cellar).

➕ J5 ✉ ul. Stradomska 11 ☎ 12 292 2212
🕐 Daily 10am–last customer

KLEZMER-HOIS (€)

klezmer.pl

Straightforward Jewish-style food is on the menu in one of the first and jolliest *klezmer* restaurants, but it may not be for you if you don't like big groups. There's music nightly, but book ahead.

➕ K6 ✉ ul. Szeroka 6 ☎ 12 411 1245
🕐 Daily 9am–10pm 🚋 Tram to ul. Miodowa

KUCHNIA U DOROTY (€)

Tasty, plain Polish cooking makes this a good place to refuel.

➕ J6 ✉ ul. Augustiańska 4 ☎ 517 945 338
🕐 Daily 10–9 🚋 Tram to plac Wolnica

NOLIO (€€)

nolio.pl

Probably the best Italian restaurant in town, Nolio serves authentic Neapolitan pizza and much more. Reserve ahead.

➕ J6 ✉ ul. Krakowska 27 ☎ 12 346 2449
🕐 Tue–Thu 4–10, Fri 4–11, Sat 1–11, Sun 1–10

NOVA KROVA (€)

novakrova.com.pl

Meat-free burgers packed with nutritious ingredients are the main draw at this vegetarian eatery.

➕ J6 ✉ plac Wolnica 3 ☎ 530 305 304
🕐 Mon–Thu 12–9, Fri–Sat 12–11, Sun 10–9
🚋 Tram to plac Wolnica

ONCE UPON A TIME IN KAZIMIERZ (€)

dawnotemu.nakazimierzu.pl

One of the sights of the area, with a mock facade of old Kazimierz shops, this restaurant is more about the atmosphere than the food. It takes the local obsession with lace tablecloths to new heights.

➕ K6 ✉ 1 ul. Szeroka ☎ 12 421 2117
🕐 Daily 10am–10.30pm 🚋 Tram to ul. Miodowa

YOUMIKO SUSHI (€€)

horairestaurant.pl

This tiny sushi bar serves top-quality dishes, including vegetarian and gluten-free options, that are fresh and tasty. Sunday is vegan day. It is very popular, so make a reservation.

➕ J6 ✉ ul. Józefa 2 ☎ 48 666 471 176
🕐 Sun–Thu 1.30–9, Fri–Sat 1.30–10

JEWISH FOOD

It's not the same as kosher, at least not in Krakow. There are only a couple of places in the city (Holiday Inn and Hotel Eden) serving kosher food, and you'll need to order well in advance. Restaurants in Kazimierz tend to serve a nostalgic kind of Jewish cuisine, but it makes a nice change from the standard Polish fare.

Beyond the Planty

When there's so much to see in the Old Town and Kazimierz, it's tempting not to wander beyond the Planty, but you'll find a variety of sights within walking distance outside the heart of the city.

Top 25

Muzeum Dom Mehoffera **88**

Muzeum Narodowe w Krakowie **90**

Schindler's Krakow **92**

More to See **94**

Where to Eat **96**

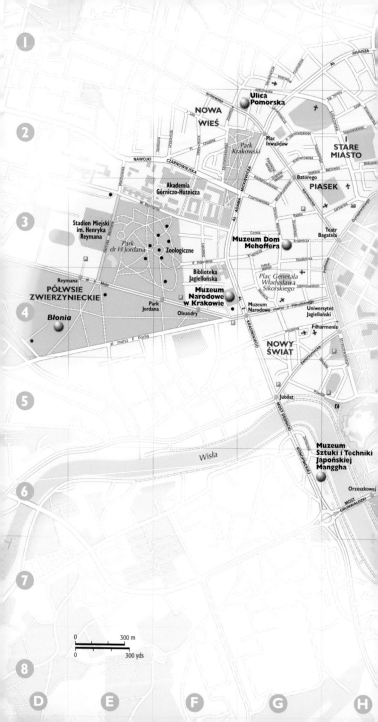

I

2

3

4

5

6

7

8

D   **E**   **F**   **G**   **H**

AL. JULIUSZA

Ulica Pomorska

NOWA WIEŚ

Park Krakowski

Plac Inwalidów

STARE MIASTO

NAWOJKI   CZARNOWIEJSKA

Akademia Górniczo-Hutnicza

Batorego

PIASEK

Stadion Miejski im. Henryka Reymana

Park dr H Jordana

Zoologiczne

Teatr Bagatela

Muzeum Dom Mehoffera

Biblioteka Jagiellońska

Plac Generała Władysława Sikorskiego

Reymana

PÓŁWSIE ZWIERZYNIECKIE

Park Jordana

Muzeum Narodowe w Krakowie

Oleandry

Muzeum Narodowe

Uniwersytet Jagielloński

Błonia

AL. KRASIŃSKIEGO

NOWY ŚWIAT

Filharmonia

Jubilat

MOST DĘBNICKI

Wisła

Muzeum Sztuki i Techniki Japońskiej Manggha

KONFEDERACKA

Orzeszkowej

MOST GRUNWALDZKI

0   300 m

0   300 yds

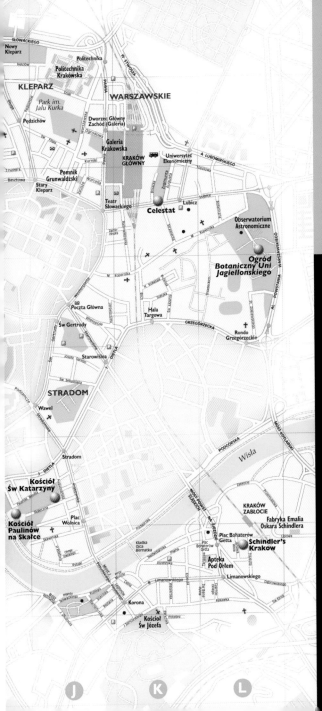

SŁOWACKIEGO

Nowy
Kleparz

Helclów

Politechnika

**Politechnika
Krakówska**

W. STWOSZA

PAWIA

KLEPARZ

*Park im.
Jalu Kurka*

WARSZAWSKIE

Pędzichów

Dworzec Główny
Zachód (Galeria)

Ogrodowa

kurniki

**Galeria
Krakowska**

**KRAKÓW
GŁÓWNY**

Uniwersytet
Ekonomiczny

R. LUBOMIRSKIEGO

Bosacka

Topolowa

3 Lipca

Basztowa

**Pomnik
Grunwaldzki**
**Stary
Kleparz**

Worcella

Teatr
Słowackiego

Szlak

Zygmunta
Wróblewskiego

Celestat

Lubicz

Lubicz

Rakowicka

M. Kopernika

WARSZAWSKIEGO

Zamknięta

**Obserwatorium
Astronomiczne**

M. Kopernika

**Ogród
Botaniczny Uni
Jagiellonskiego**

AL. POWSTANIA WARSZAWSKIEGO

Poczta Główna

Wielopole

Dietla

Św Gertrudy

**Hala
Targowa**

Starowiślna

GRZEGÓRZECKA

Józefa Dietla

Św Sebastiana

Św. Gertrudy

DIETLA

**Rondo
Grzegórzeckie**

STRADOM

Wawel

MOSTOWA

POWIŚLE

PODGÓRSKA

Wisła

MOSTU KOTLARSKIEGO

Stradom

J. DIETLA

PODGÓRSKA

MOST POWSTAŃCÓW ŚLĄSKICH

**Kościół
Św Katarzyny**

Plac
Wolnica

NA ZJEŹDZIE

**KRAKÓW
ZABŁOCIE**

Lipowa

**Kościół
Paulinów
na Skałce**

Krakusa

Kładka
Ojca
Bernatka

Plac Bohaterów
Getta

**Fabryka Emalia
Oskara Schindlera**

**Schindler's
Krakow**

Rybaki

Plac
Bohaterów
Getta

**Apteka
Pod Orłem**

Limanowskiego

Dąbrowskiego

Planty
Nowackiego

Korona

Limanowskiego

Krakówka

Św Kinga

**Kościół
Św Józefa**

Potebni

J **K** **L**

Muzeum Dom Mehoffera

● 14th-century wood carving of Virgin Mary on a lion
● Portrait of the artist's wife, Florentine, painted on their honeymoon
● *Roman Epic*, Mehoffer's favorite landscape
● Art nouveau stained-glass panel, *Vita Somnium Breve*

TIP

● After taking in the house and paintings, head out into the garden to relax. It's an oasis of peace and quiet away from the bustling city.

The house of the Modernist artist Józef Mehoffer, restored to how it was when he lived there, gives an insight into the life of one of the leading lights of the Young Poland movement.

Acclaimed artist Coming to prominence at the turn of the 20th century, Mehoffer founded the art group Sztuka with several other leading fin-de-siècle painters. A notable art figure on the European stage—he designed stained glass for Fribourg cathedral in Switzerland—he was an admired rector of Krakow's Academy of Fine Arts and contributed to the influential arts journals of the day.

Home and studio Already well established as a painter, printmaker, artist in stained glass and interior designer by the time he bought the house in 1930, Mehoffer lived and worked

Clockwise from far left: The drawing room; view of the garden from the house; the house seen from the back garden; painting of Krakow's Market Square by Józef Mehoffer in 1903; butterfly curtains—a replica of Mehoffer's original design; detail of Mehoffer's stained glass

here until he died in 1946, nurturing his garden and entertaining his fellow artists and intellectuals in the Young Poland movement.

Creative life Visiting the house, you begin to get an idea of Krakow's flourishing art scene between the wars. Mehoffer was a collector as well as an artist. Like Feliks "Manggha" Jasieński, he enjoyed Japanese art, but he also admired and collected Chinese and Breton ceramics, Jewish art, fine furniture and tapestries. Sadly, many of his finest pieces were seized by the Nazis and never returned.

The many portraits on the walls show other significant artists living in Krakow at the time, such as Jan Matejko, who collaborated with Mehoffer and Wyspiański on renovations to St. Mary's Church at the end of the 19th century. Such figures would have dined and debated with Mehoffer here.

THE BASICS

mnk.pl

➕ G3

✉ ul. Krupnicza 26

☎ 12 421 1143,
12 423 2079

🕐 Tue–Sun 10–4

🍴 Café/restaurant
Meho-Cafe (€) with
summer garden

♿ None

💷 Inexpensive

Muzeum Narodowe w Krakowie

HIGHLIGHTS

● Wyspiański's designs for stained glass in Wawel Cathedral
● Krakow stained glass from the 13th, 14th and 15th centuries
● 10th-century silver Włocławek goblet
● 17th-century Persian belt

TIP

● Buy a combined ticket to see all three permanent exhibitions for little more than the price of two.

The top floor of the main building of the National Museum in Krakow has the largest collection of 20th-century Polish art in the city, drawing together all the big names you'll find mentioned on your visits to the main sights.

Century of the new The 20th century was a period of great change in Poland. After independence in 1920, there was a new mood of confidence. Building on the earlier work of Modernist artists, such as Witkiewicz, a philosopher, novelist, playwright and visual artist, Poland's 20th-century artists engaged with thinkers from beyond their own country and expressed new ideas with vigor. Most of the permanent exhibition, which mainly comprises art made after 1945, shows a revival of the struggle for independence, including some

From left: museum entrance; the top floor of the main building of the National Museum in Krakow focuses on 20th-century Polish art

interesting pieces by Tadeusz Kantor, the world-famous Krakow artist and playwright.

Domestic arts One floor below the modern art collection, a display of decorative arts and crafts spans the millennium from the 11th century onward, with beautiful early pieces of silverware, stained glass and embroidery, mainly sourced from local churches. Examples of 20th-century Polish crafts display the distinctive traditional styles.

Objects of war The ground-floor exhibition Weapons and Colors in Poland presents another great contrast, with military hardware from the Middle Ages to World War II. Exhibits include a wide variety of arms, armor and the uniforms of Polish military units from the 18th century onward.

THE BASICS

mnk.pl

🔲 F4

✉ 1 al. 3 Maja

☎ 012 295 5500

🕐 Tue–Fri 9–5, Sat 10–6, Sun 10–4

🍴 Café (€)

🚌 109, 124, 134, 144, 152. Tram 20

♿ Very good, elevators, ramps and wheelchair hoists

🎟 Inexpensive; Sun permanent exhibitions free

Schindler's Krakow

HIGHLIGHTS

● Apteka Pod Orłem
● Memorial in plac Bohaterów Getta—the empty chairs symbolize the ghetto after the liquidation
● Ghetto walls
● Schindler's Emalia factory

The events in Steven Spielberg's Oscar-winning movie *Schindler's List*, based on the true story of a factory owner who saved more than 1,000 Jews from the Nazis, happened here, in Podgórze.

DID YOU KNOW?

● Spielberg's movie was based on the novel *Schindler's Ark* by Thomas Keneally.

The ghetto In 1941, the occupying Nazis forced Krakow's 20,000 or so remaining Jews into just 320 buildings in a new ghetto in Podgórze. Forced labor and overcrowding soon took their toll. Deportations to the death camps began in 1942, and in 1943 the ghetto was liquidated, its remaining inhabitants murdered in the streets. You can see the remains of ghetto walls on ul. Lwowska and ul. Limanowskiego across the Postańców Śląskich bridge from Kazimierz.

TIP

● There's a useful plan of the immediate area on the corner outside the Apteka Pod Orłem.

The pharmacy One Christian business remained in the ghetto. The pharmacy Apteka

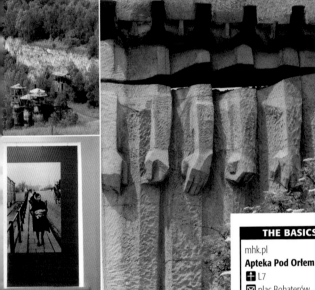

Clockwise from far left: Empty chair sculptures on plac Bohaterów Getta; view of the Nazi labor camp at Płaszów; memorial at Płaszów; exhibition at the Pharmacy "under the Eagle"; the original ghetto walls

Pod Orłem (Pharmacy "under the Eagle"), was run by Tadeusz Pankiewicz, who actively helped Jews resist and escape the Nazis. Today it houses a small exhibition on life and death in the ghetto. It also shows films and photographs of prewar life, when Jews made up a quarter of the population of Krakow.

The factory owner Negoatiating with the authorities, Oskar Schindler found work in his enamel factory for Jews who would otherwise have been taken to the nearby camp at Płaszów. By later transferring his factory to the Sudetenland he managed to rescue more than 1,000 Jewish men and women from certain death. Today, you can see the outside of Schindler's former Emalia factory at ul. Lipowa 4 (down ul. Kącik and under the railway). Now part of the Krakow History Museum, it houses an exhibition on the Nazi occupation.

THE BASICS

mhk.pl

Apteka Pod Orlem

➕ L7

✉ plac Bohaterów Getta 18

☎ 12 656 5625

🕐 Mon 10–2, Tue–Sun 9–5

🚋 Tram 3, 9, 19 to plac Bohaterów Getta

♿ Good

💶 Inexpensive, Mon free; audio guide inexpensive

Schindler's Factory

mhk.pl

➕ M7

✉ ul. Lipowa 4

☎ 12 257 1017

🕐 Apr–Oct Mon 10–4, Tue–Sun 10–8; Nov–Mar Mon 10–2, Tue–Sun 10–6

🚋 Tram 7, 11, 20 to Zabłocie

💶 Inexpensive

More to See

BŁONIA

When the celebration is too great to be contained in Rynek Główny, Cracovians take to the great 48ha (120-acre) Błonia meadow. Gifted to the Norbertine nuns in 1172, the land was used to graze cattle in medieval times. From the 19th century, it was the site of grand military parades, and was also where Poland's first football match was held in 1894. More recently, Pope John Paul II said Mass and canonized saints here several times. It's a good place to come for a picnic and kick a ball or fly a kite.

➕ D4 ✉ Between al. 3 Maja and ul. Reymonta 🚌 109, 124, 134, 144 to Cracovia Hotel. Tram 20 to Cracovia Hotel

CELESTAT

mhk.pl

This uniquely Cracovian institution will only make sense if you have visited the city walls. This is the headquarters of the Marksmen's Guild, known as the Bratstwo Kurkowe, or Brotherhood of the Cockerel, who for centuries have been the city's ace sharpshooters. Here you'll find a rifle range and a museum of the guild's history, with pride of place given to a Renaissance silver cockerel.

➕ K3 ✉ ul. Lubicz 16 ☎ 12 429 3791 🕐 May–Oct Tue, Thu–Sat and second Sun of month 9.30–5, Wed 9–4; Nov–Apr Tue–Wed, Fri–Sat, second Sun of month 9–4, Thu 11–6 💰 Inexpensive; includes admission to Barbican and city walls

KOŚCIÓŁ PAULINÓW NA SKAŁCE

skalka.paulini.pl

The steps of the Church on the Rock are where St. Stanisław was murdered in 1079" allegedly for clashing with the king, Bolesław the Bold. St. Stanisław's statue outside the baroque church overlooks a pool of holy water into which the saint's severed finger fell. Eminent Poles, including writer and painter Wyspiański and the Nobel Prize-winning poet Czesław Miłosz are buried in the crypt.

Muzeum Sztuki i Techniki Japońskiej Manggha

H6 ✉ ul. Skałeczna 15 ☎ 12 421 7244 🕑 Church and crypt Apr–Oct Mon–Sat 9–12, 1–5, Sun 10–12, 1–5 🚊 Tram 6, 8, 10, 13 to plac Wolnica 💷 Free

KOŚCIÓŁ ŚW. KATARZYNY

Fire, flood and earthquakes have rocked St. Catherine's church since it was founded by Kazimierz the Great in the 14th century. A good example of Krakow Gothic, its interior is a gallery of styles down the ages, including early baroque altars, a 15th-century statue of the Virgin Mary and 15th-century murals in the adjoining cloisters.

J6 ✉ ul. Augustiańska 7 ☎ 12 430 6242 🕑 Daily, first service 6am, last 7pm 🚊 Tram 6, 8, 10, 13 to plac Wolnica 💷 Free

MUZEUM SZTUKI I TECHNIKI JAPOŃSKIEJ MANGGHA

manggha.krakow.pl

Named for Feliks "Manggha" Jasieński and founded by the movie director Andrzej Wajda to display the connoisseur's collection of Japanese art, the Museum of Japanese Art and Technology Manggha is a striking piece of contemporary architecture by the Vistula. It has a splendid collection of Japanese woodcuts, handicrafts, weaponry and porcelain, as well as a good sushi restaurant.

G6 ✉ ul. Konopnickiej 26 ☎ 12 267 2703, 12 267 3753 🕑 Tue–Sun 10–6 🍴 Restaurant 🚊 Tram 1, 2, 6 to Jubilat/ Most Dębnicki 💷 Moderate

OGRÓD BOTANICZNY

ogrod.uj.edu.pl

The Jagiellonian University's Botanical Gardens are Poland's oldest and largest, first laid out in 1783. Though not extensive, they are a relaxing haven just 15 minutes' walk from the city center. Investigate the Jubilee glasshouse wrapped around a group of palms several floors high—stairs take you level with the treetops.

L3 ✉ ul. Mikołaja Kopernika 27 ☎ 12 663 3624 🕑 Mid-Apr–Oct 9–7 (Oct 9–5); glasshouses Sat–Thu 10–6 (Oct 10–4) 💷 Inexpensive

ULICA POMORSKA

mhk.pl

This plain, former student residence was used by the Gestapo during World War II as a center for detention and torture. The cells are preserved, and there is also a good permanent exhibition on Krakow 1939–56 with photographs and memorabilia of the resistance. The place has a powerful atmosphere.

G2 ✉ ul. Pomorska 2 ☎ 12 633 1414 🕑 Apr–Oct Tue–Sat 10–5.30; Nov–Mar Tue–Wed, Fri 9–4, Thu 12–7, Sat–Sun 10–5 🚊 Tram 4, 8, 13, 14 to plac Inwalidów 💷 Inexpensive

Lily pads at the Botanical Gardens

Where to Eat

BAL (€)

A great stop-off after visiting Schindler's Factory, this stylishly utilitarian place has minimalist decor, a blackboard menu and a clientele of clutter-hating design types. The menu includes soup, quiche, sandwiches and coffee, providing a respite from the medieval meat-and-kitsch of the Old Town eating scene.

➕ M6 ✉ ul. Ślusarska 9 ☎ 604 814 484
🕐 Mon–Sat 8.30am–10pm, Sun 8.30am–9pm

CAFÉ SZAFÉ (€)

cafeszafe.com

A bright, cozy, quirkily decorated café, Szafé also hosts music and all sorts of arts events. It's a popular expat hangout. You can get good coffee and cake, too.

➕ G4 ✉ ul. Felicjanek 10 ☎ 663 905 652
🕐 Mon–Fri 9am–1am, Sat–Sun 10am–midnight

CHATA (€)

polskakuchnia.com.pl

Tasty Polish dishes are served in a typical rustic interior with wooden beams and brick walls. The menu also offers big "feasts"—a selection of dishes for several people to share.

➕ H2 ✉ ul. Krowoderska 21 ☎ 888 101 100 🕐 Daily 1–11

DYNIA (€)

dynia.krakow.pl

There's a warm welcome from the friendly staff in this brick-walled restaurant, with a courtyard for outdoor eating in summer. Come for breakfast, sandwiches, lots of grills or the carefully calorie-counted "fitness menu." The kitchen closes an hour before the bar.

➕ J3 ✉ ul. Krupnicza 20 ☎ 12 430 0838
🕐 Mon–Fri 8am–11pm, Sat–Sun 9am–11pm

EUSKADI (€)

The only (and tiny) Basque restaurant in Krakow, Euskadi is seriously good, offering skilfully prepared dishes in tapas-like portions (*pintxos*) as well as steaks and seafood, accompanied by quality wines.

➕ K7 ✉ ul. Brodzińskiego 4 ☎ 48 535 484 056 🕐 Daily 12–10

PLAŻA KRAKÓW (€€)

plazakrakow.com.pl

Most visitors don't come to Krakow to lounge on the beach, but the Krakow Beach complex on the Vistula south of Kazimierz has a stretch of sand, a nightclub and this sassy, modern restaurant.

➕ H7 ✉ ul. Ludwinowska 2 ☎ 530 950 303
🕐 Daily 11–11

ZAKŁADKA (€)

zakladkabistro.pl

This Polish-French bistro serves good, plain food in an unpretentious setting.

➕ F6 ✉ ul. Józefińska 2 ☎ 12 422 7442
🕐 Mon 5–10, Tue–Thu 12–10, Fri–Sat 12–11, Sun 12–9

FOOD STALLS

The stalls at Stary Kleparz, though scarcely a couple of minutes' walk beyond the Planty, are a world away from the tourist-pleasing wares of the Sukiennice. But there's also good bread, sausages and cheese, so it's the ideal place to assemble a picnic. Good buys are local honey and strings of dried wild mushrooms.

➕ H2 ✉ ul. Krowoderska 22 ☎ 12 634 1532, starykleparz.com 🕐 Mon–Sat 7–7

Farther Afield

If you only have a couple of days in Krakow, you may choose to make one of these trips with a tour company, but they are all easy to reach by public transport. However you travel, any one will add a different dimension to your visit to the city.

Top 25

Auschwitz-Birkenau **100**

Kopalnia Soli Wieliczka **102**

More to See **104**

Excursions **105**

Entertainment and Nightlife **106**

Where to Eat **106**

Auschwitz-Birkenau

HIGHLIGHTS

● Gate with the motto
"Arbeit Macht Frei"
● Film of the camp's
liberation
● Heaps of prisoners'
effects: shoes, spectacles,
suitcases
● Mounds of hair shorn
from prisoners
● Birkenau barracks,
unloading ramp, railway
● Ruins of gas chambers
and crematoria
● Moving photographs

**Many visitors to Krakow feel they must
see the Nazi concentration camp, but
consider whether it's the right time for
you to go. It's a powerful, emotional
experience and maybe not something
to slot casually into a city break.**

TIPS

● You cannot know
whether the person next to
you lost a relative or even
their whole family in the
camp. It's important to be
respectful—particularly of
the "no photographs" rule.
● Visits are not recom-
mended for under-14s.

Extermination camp The Nazis brought the
first slave laborers, mainly Polish political prisoners, to Auschwitz in 1940. Many soon died
because of the appalling conditions working for
the German industries that relocated here; others starved to death, were executed or died
from torture or medical experiments. In 1941,
Soviet prisoners of war were brought to the
extermination camp at nearby Birkenau. By
1942, the camp was receiving Jews from all
over Europe and became one of the main sites

Clockwise from far left: The entrance to Auschwitz, with "Arbeit Macht Frei" ("Work Sets You Free") above the gates; the main SS guardhouse at Birkenau, known as the Death Gate; part of the Extermination exhibition; sleeping quarters in the quarantine block at Birkenau

THE BASICS

auschwitz.org

✚ See map ▷ 98

✉ ul. Więźniów Oświęcimia 20, Oświęcim

☎ 33 844 8099 (Mon–Fri 7–3)

🕐 Site of the camp Dec–Feb daily 8–3; Mar, Nov 8–4; Apr, Oct 8–5; May, Sep 8–6; Jun–Aug 8–7; advance booking essential

🍴 Cafeteria (€)

🚉 Oświęcim

🚌 Oświęcim train station, then one of several local buses to the Auschwitz site. Shuttle bus runs between Auschwitz and Birkenau (3km/2 miles) mid-Apr to Oct

♿ Few; flat site but not all the museum is accessible

📷 Museum free; headphones, film, inexpensive; English-language guided group tours of 3 hours 30 min moderate (book ahead); longer study tours

of the Nazi drive to wipe out the Jewish race. Unloaded after days traveling in cattle trucks, those judged unfit to work were ordered into "shower rooms"—gas chambers that killed up to 2,000 at a time. It is estimated that between 1 and 1.5 million people died here before the camp was liberated in 1945.

Lessons of history Auschwitz is now a living memorial to those who died here and to the horror of the Final Solution. The museum at Auschwitz has piles of personal possessions taken from the prisoners. In the barracks at Birkenau the wooden bunks would collapse under the weight of the many prisoners crowded into each one. You'll also find the remnants of the gas chambers and crematoria. The ashes of the dead still lie in the ground here.

Kopalnia Soli Wieliczka

HIGHLIGHTS

● St. Kinga's Chapel
● Warsaw Chamber
● Pieskowa Skała Chamber
● Erazm Barącz Chamber
● Weimar Chamber
● 36m-high (118ft)
Stanisław Staszic Chamber

DID YOU KNOW?

● Many famous people have visited the salt mines, from the poet Goethe onward. More recent celebrities include George Bush Senior, Britain's Prince Edward and Ritchie Blackmore of the band Deep Purple.

● The underground micro-climate is helpful for people with respiratory problems and the mine runs its own treatment center (see website for details).

TIP

● Visitors have to wait until there is a group of 35 for a tour in their own language. In practice, this wait is never longer than an hour and often shorter. At quiet times of year, call or check the website for times of English-language tours.

A visit to a salt mine may sound grim, but this is a great half-day out from Krakow. The jaws of more than a million people a year drop when they see the vast underground chambers.

Grey gold There have been saltworks at Wieliczka since neolithic times, but mining and the sale of the valuable rock salt began in earnest in the 11th century, with the oldest known shaft in the mine dating back to the 13th century. The wealth salt brought to Krakow belonged to its rulers. In medieval times it made up about a third of royal revenue and paid for much of the rich architecture you see in the city today. Commercial mining has now stopped and the mine is a tourist attraction.

Clockwise from far left: The top of the Daniłowicz shaft; the Great Chamber; salt sculptures carved by the miners; St. Kinga's Chapel

Going deep The hardest part of the two-and-a-half-hour tour is the first descent, a walk down 378 steps. After that it's an easy, spacious, well-lit route, covering about 2km (1 mile). The deepest you go is 135m (443ft) below ground level. The mine is much more extensive than this, however: it goes down to 327m (1,073ft) with nearly 3,000 chambers on nine levels. The Daniłowicz shaft used by visitors was first sunk in 1635 and reaches down to 243m (797ft). As well as seeing the wooden mine workings, you will see carvings and sculptures made by the miners in the salt, underground lakes and huge ornate chambers used for all sorts of events, from weddings to orchestral concerts. A lift brings you back to the surface at the end of the tour.

THE BASICS

wieliczka-saltmine.com

➕ See map ▷ 99

✉ ul. Daniłowicza 10, Wieliczka

☎ 12 278 7302, 12 278 7366

🕐 Apr–Oct daily 7.30–7.30; Nov–Mar 8–5; Easter Sun 7.30–2.30.

🍴 Cafeteria above ground; simple restaurant at end of tour below ground (€)

🚃 Wieliczka Rynek, from Krakow main station

🚌 Wieliczka Kopalnia, bus 304 from the main bus station

♿ Excellent; $1m-worth of elevators, ramps and toilets make the most popular sections wheelchair-accessible

💰 Expensive; fee for taking pictures inexpensive

More to See

KOPIEC KOŚCIUSZKI

About 3.5km (2 miles) from the center of the city, this monument to Tadeusz Kościuszko, dating from the 1820s and restored in the 2000s, is a pleasant walk out of town on a fine day, with good views of the city along the way. There is also a small museum to the hero in the old fortifications.

🔲 B5 ✉ al. Waszyngtona 1 ☎ 12 425 1116 🕓 Daily 9–dusk; also evening opening with separate ticket May–Sep daily dusk–11pm; museum daily 9.30–4.30 🍴 Café with outside terrace (€) 🚋 Tram 1, 2, 6 to Salwator then bus 100 from Salwator, or 101 from Rondo Grunwaldzkie 🚭 Circular path to the top of the mount is steep 💷 Inexpensive; separate ticket for small wax-work museum inexpensive

LAS WOLSKI

Home to Krakow's zoo (▷ 106) and Piłsudski's Mound, this forest west of the city between ul. Królowej Jadwigi and the Vistula has eight walking routes, a winter ski route and a bike route, as well as several examples of traditional wooden architecture.

🔲 See map ▷ 99 🚌 102, 134, 152

NOWA HUTA

mhk.pl

If you are interested in seeing the Soviet Union's influence on Poland, visit this suburb, built on Stalin's orders in the 1940s. It's very spread out so allow a lot of time, or take a tour from Krakow. The Sendzimir steelworks are now owned by an Indian global industrialist, but "Our Lord's Ark," the Queen of Poland Church, built in 1977, is a dramatic symbol of Polish resistance to the Soviet way of doing things. Visit the local museum first to get your bearings.

🔲 See map ▷ 99 ✉ Museum of the History of Nowa Huta, os. Słoneczne 16 ☎ 12 425 9775 🕓 Apr–Oct Tue–Sun and second Sun of month 9.30–5; Nov–Mar Tue, Thu–Sat 9–4, Wed 10–5, second Sun of month 9–4. Closed Tue after second Sun 🚋 Tram 4 to plac Centralny 💷 Museum inexpensive, Wed free

Cycling in Las Wolski

The crucifixion in the Queen of Poland Church, Nowa Huta

Excursions

CZĘSTOCHOWA

Home of Poland's holiest shrine, Częstochowa's Jana Góra monastery is not only of interest to pilgrims but to anyone who wants to explore the people's passionate relationship with the Catholic religion and how it is entwined in the country's history.

At the heart of Jasna Góra is the icon of the Black Madonna, already several centuries old when Pauline monks first came to the "bright hill" in 1382. The scars on the Virgin's face date from a 15th-century robbery attempt. The Gothic chapel was begun shortly after, while numerous attacks led to the fortification of the hill. In 1655, a tiny number of troops and monks held off a siege by 3,000 Swedes—a miracle that inspired the rest of the conquered country to rise up and repel the invaders. The icon became a symbol of a free Poland.

THE BASICS

Distance: 140km (87 miles)
Journey time: 2–3 hours by coach from Dworzec bus station; 90 mins–2 hours by train from Dworzec Główny
🛈 al. Najświętszej Maryi Panny 65 ☎ 34 368 2250; cestochowa.pl
🕐 Mon–Sat 9–5
Jasna Góra
jasnagora.pl
✉ ul. O.A. Kordeckiego 2
☎ 34 377 7777
💰 Expensive
❓ You need to pre-book a tour to see the icon

ZAKOPANE

A winter sports and summer hiking center high in the jagged Tatra Mountains near the border with Slovakia, Poland's winter capital is also popular with visitors who just want to breathe the mountain air and sample the traditional highlander, or *góralski,* way of life.

The easiest mountain resort to reach from Krakow, and a ski resort for more than 100 years, Zakopane has also attracted Poland's great artists, including the writer and painter Stanisław Witkiewicz, who in the 1890s, designed Willa (Villa) Koliba, thereby instigating the "Zakopane style" of ornamental wooden buildings that is much copied today. The legacy is a town that has more than a century of cultural heritage, and the villa now houses the Museum of Zakopane Style.

For winter sport lovers, the town offers 50 ski lifts and 160km (100 miles) of ski runs. Hikers should take the mountain stream rushing along the main street as their starting point for exploring some of the 240km (149 miles) of marked trails in the Tatra National Park.

THE BASICS

Distance: 100km (62 miles)
Journey time: 2 hours or more by bus from Dworzec bus station depending on traffic; 2.5–3.5 hours by train from Dworzec Główny
Willa Koliba
✉ ul. Kościelska 18 ☎ 18 201 3602; muzeumtatrzanskie.pl
🕐 Wed–Sat 9–5, Sun 9–3
💰 Inexpensive
Tatrzański Park Narodowy (Tatra National Park Office)
tpn.pl
✉ ul. Kuźnice 1 ☎ 18 202 3300

Entertainment and Nightlife

AQUA PARK
parkwodny.pl
The biggest indoor aqua park in Poland, to the northeast of Krakow center, boasts pipes and slides, the Rapid River and a sauna, as well as lane swimming, and climbing walls for dry fun.
✉ ul. Dobrego Pasterza 126 ☎ 12 616 3190 🕐 Daily 8am–10pm 🍴 Restaurant (€) 🚌 128 🎫 Moderate

GOLF
krakow-valley.com
This 18-hole championship golf course to the northwest of the city offers a driving range, shooting range, horse riding and skiing in winter.

✉ 328 Miejscowość Paczółtowice, 32-063 Krzeszowice ☎ 12 258 6000 🕐 Daily 🚌 Paczółtowice 🎫 Expensive

KRAKOW ZOO
zoo-krakow.pl
Set in the middle of Las Wolski, the 17ha (42-acre) zoo has raised litters of snow leopards, Chinese leopards, jaguars and pythons. Other rare animals include pygmy hippopotamuses and Przewalski horses, which are extinct in the wild. There's also a petting zoo.
✉ ul. Kasy Oszczędności Miasta Krakowa 14 ☎ 12 425 3551 🕐 Summer daily 9–7; spring and fall 9–4; winter 9–3 🚌 134 from Cracovia Hotel 🎫 Moderate

Where to Eat

CHATA ZBÓJNICKA (€)
chatazbojnicka.pl
This rustic hideaway offers a log fire in winter, a garden in summer and hearty *góralski* (mountain) cooking all year.
✉ ul. Jagiellońska, Zakopane ☎ 18 201 4217 🕐 Daily 5pm–midnight

KARCZMA CZARCI JAR (€)
czarcijar.pl
Expect Polish and traditional *góralski* dishes at this rustic pine cabin. You'll be serenaded by a highland band.

✉ ul. Małe Żywczańskie 11a, Zakopane ☎ 18 206 4178 🕐 Daily 1–11

KARCZMA OBROCHTÓWKA (€)
Enjoy well-prepared traditional highland dishes in a traditional Zakopane inn. There is a summer garden and an evening folk band.
✉ ul. Kraszewskiego 10a, Zakopane ☎ 18 206 2979 🕐 Daily 12–10

KARCZMA SABAŁA (€€)
sabala.zakopane.pl
Named after a famous folk singer and housed in a century-old hotel on Zakopane's main street, Sabała has old wooden ceilings and a terrace. The menu features both highland and international dishes.
✉ ul. Krupówki 11, Zakopane ☎ 18 201 5092 🕐 Daily 11am–midnight

With a tradition of welcoming guests that stretches back centuries, Krakow knows about hospitality. Some of the grand old hotels have been renovated, but you'll also find a choice of good budget hotels.

Introduction **108**
Budget Hotels **109**
Mid-Range Hotels **110**
Luxury Hotels **112**

Introduction

Since the city is popular year-round, try to book your hotel as much in advance as possible. You'll discover a wide variety of accommodations, from smart modern chain hotels to hostels and simple, sparsely furnished apartments, with a range of good-value places in between.

Sleep with history

For the first-time visitor it makes sense to try to stay in or near the Old Town so that all the sights are within easy reach. As an alternative, visitors interested in Jewish history might want to consider Kazimierz, where new hotels, guest houses and tourist apartments are opening all the time, although the district cannot match the Old Town's luxurious renovated palaces or the facilities of the large, purpose-built hotels that ring the Planty. The young and fashionable also like Kazimierz because of its indie bars and clubs and cutting-edge atmosphere, even if it is crumbling around the edges a little bit.

Local streets

Even beyond the Planty, you may be in easy walking distance of the center and its sights. What you lose by not having a museum on your doorstep you might gain from not having a hip cellar bar disgorging rowdy revelers into your street in the early hours. Public transportation is good and easy to negotiate and taxis are inexpensive, so if you do find yourself outside the central districts—perhaps staying in student accommodations on the city outskirts during the summer vacation—do not despair. You will still be able to get back from the nightclub, by nightbus if need be.

PRICES
Note that even hotels that quote prices in euros will expect to be paid in zloty at the current rate of exchange. If you stay longer than one night, your bill will include a small tourist tax.

From top: Hotel Eden; a hotel restaurant; bath treats at Hotel Copernicus; the rooftop terrace at Hotel Stary

Budget Hotels

PRICES
Expect to pay up to 250PLN (€75) a night for a double room in a budget hotel.

CRACOW B&B

cracowbb.com

Crisp, modern and spotlessly clean, this B&B near the main railway station is a great budget choice, with its parquet floors, huge rooms and breakfast in bed. There's a kitchen for guest use, with free tea and coffee. The only downside is the shared bathroom.

➕ M2 ✉ ul. Moniuszki 24 ☎ 604 903 733 🚊 Tram to Rondo Mogilska

CYBULSKIEGO GUEST ROOMS

freerooms.pl

Arranged in apartments with private shower rooms and kitchen facilities, the 14 plainly furnished beds here would suit anyone on a budget who needs more privacy than hostels provide. You get your own front door key, helpful staff, excellent WiFi, and a good buffet breakfast.

➕ G3 ✉ ul. Cybulskiego 6 ☎ 12 423 0532

HOTEL GRAND FELIX

hotelgrandfelix.pl

For a different take on Krakow, stay at this 50-room business hotel in Nowa Huta. It's bland but comfortable, and only a tram ride away from the city.

➕ Off map ✉ os. Złotej Jesieni 12 ☎ 12 681 8600 🚊 Tram to Rondo Hipokratesa

IBIS KRAKOW CENTRUM

ibishotel.com

Close to the Vistula and Wawel, but without views, and 10 minutes' walk from the Old Town, this is an efficiently run chain hotel with 175 rooms. There's a summer beer garden.

➕ G5 ✉ ul. Syrokomil 2 ☎ 12 299 3300 🚊 Tram 2 to Jubilat ♿ 6 adapted rooms

KLEZMER-HOIS

klezmer.pl

Budget travelers will be interested in the four rooms on the second floor of this 10-room hotel near the Remuh Synagogue. They have been neatly renovated, though only two have their own bathroom. The restaurant downstairs (▷ 84) is one of Kazimierz's best Jewish eateries.

➕ K5 ✉ ul. Szeroka 6 ☎ 12 411 1245 🚊 Tram 2 to Rakowicka

MARIE CURIE

Only bookable through popular booking websites, this rambling guest house has modern, well-maintained rooms but no reception (you need a code to enter, which is emailed to you). The big plus is the location near the Old Town and the main station.

➕ J3 ✉ ul. Marie Curie Skłodowskiej 🚊 Tram to Dworzec Główny

PIANO GUEST HOUSE

pianoguesthouse.com

Inexpensive guest house near the main station, with friendly owners, a stylish breakfast room and basic but clean and comfortable rooms. Breakfast included and tours available.

➕ K1 ✉ ul. Kątowa ☎ 12 632 1371 🚊 Tram 2 to Rakowicka

VIENNA HOUSE

vi-hotels.com

This large, three-star chain hotel just outside the historical center has rooms fitted out with everything the traveler needs on the road.

➕ M3 ✉ Przy Rondzie 2 ☎ 12 299 0000 🚊 Tram to Rondo Mogilska

Mid-Range Hotels

> **PRICES**
>
> Expect to pay between 250PLN (€75) and 500PLN (€150) a night for a double room in a mid-range hotel.

ART HOTEL NIEBIESKI
niebieski.com.pl

Half the 13 rooms in this elegant old building near the Salwator monastery have views over the Vistula and Wawel Hill. Bathrooms have heated floors and showers and it's all decorated in modern Polish romantic style. There's a spa to unwind in, and underground parking.

➕ F6 ✉ ul. Flisacka 3 ☎ 12 297 4000
🚋 Tram 1, 2, 6 to Salwator

FRANCUSKI HOTEL
hotel-francuski.com

Madly modern when it first opened in 1912, this 42-room honeymooners' favorite near St. Florian's Gate has a grand fin-de-siècle feel, while the facilities, including wellness center and WiFi, are up to date. Parking, children and even pets welcome.

➕ J3 ✉ ul. Pijarska 13 ☎ 666 195 831

GOLDEN TULIP KAZIMIERZ

This friendly and comfortable hotel with 139 rooms is central but surprisingly quiet. It is located in the heart of Kazimierz, within walking distance of Wawel Castle and the Old Town.

➕ J6 ✉ ul. Krakowska 28 ☎ 12 424 4800

HOTEL AMADEUS
hotel-amadeus.pl

Tucked away near the Mały Rynek, this 14th-century town house with a 17th-century St. Mary of the Rosary painted on its facade has welcomed princes, ambassadors and the dancer Mikhail Barishnikov. The 22 traditionally styled rooms have modern facilities including Jacuzzi baths. There is a fitness room, sauna and car parking.

➕ J4 ✉ ul. Mikołajska 20 ☎ 12 429 6070

HOTEL EDEN
hoteleden.pl

On the Kazimierz site where, legend has it, the founder of the Izaak Synagogue discovered treasure in his garden, this hotel has deep Jewish roots. The 27 characterless rooms have modern facilities, and there is also a sauna, salt grotto and ritual Mikvah bath (open to nonguests and said to be the only one in Poland) on site. The restaurant serves kosher food.

➕ K6 ✉ ul. Ciemna 15 ☎ 12 430 6565

HOTEL ESTER
hotel-ester.krakow.pl

Right in the center of Kazimierz, overlooking the Remuh, Popper and Old synagogues, this traditional hotel with 32 rooms has a restaurant with live *klezmer* music on weekends.

➕ K5 ✉ ul. Szeroka 20 ☎ 12 429 1188

HOTEL KARMEL
karmel.com.pl

In Kazimierz, between ul. Szeroka and plac Nowy, the Karmel has 11 traditionally styled bedrooms in a 19th-century building with an Italian restaurant in its aged cellar.

➕ K6 ✉ ul. Kupa 15 ☎ 12 430 6697
🚋 Tram 3, 9, 24 to ul. Miodowa

HOTEL POLLERA
pollera.com.pl

Just across the Planty from the main station, this very well-appointed and characterful hotel has been in business since 1834. The elegant rooms have antique-style furniture, and all have their

own (slightly dated) bathrooms. The high-ceilinged restaurant is used only for breakfast, or you can ask for croissants and coffee in your room.

🔲 J3 🔲 ul. Szpitalna 30 ☎ 12 422 1044

HOTEL SASKI

hotelsaski.com.pl

A few steps off the Rynek Główny, this grande dame of Krakow's hotel scene is the place to head for a bit of Central European style without the crippling bill at check-out. While the styling of the building is all art nouveau, rooms are fairly standard and some don't have their own bathrooms.

🔲 H3 🔲 ul. Sławkowska 3 ☎ 12 421 4222

HOTEL SENACKI

hotelsenacki.pl

Opposite the church of św. Piotra i Pawła and a 24-hour supermarket on the Royal Route to Wawel, this 20-room hotel in a 14th-century house is traditionally decorated. There is a café-bar in the 13th-century cellar and a restaurant with a venerable beamed ceiling and carved stone pillars. The staff are knowledgeable and very helpful.

🔲 H4 🔲 ul. Grodzka 51 ☎ 12 422 7686

NOVOTEL

novotel.com

Right on the river but still an easy walk from the Old Town, this contemporary hotel is well designed. There are 198 rooms as well as a separate executive floor. Downstairs, the children's play corner is within easy sight of the lobby-bar. Many bedrooms have a Wawel view. Other facilities include a garden brasserie, pool, Jacuzzi, sauna, gym and spa center.

🔲 G5 🔲 ul. Tadeusza Kościuszki 5 ☎ 12 299 2900

POD WAWELEM

hotelpodwawelem.pl

This is a cool place to stay in a stunning location, between the Sheraton and Wawel Hill on the banks of the Vistula. There are 48 contemporary-style rooms sandwiched between a rooftop café-bar with exceptional views and a cellar bar.

🔲 G5 🔲 plac Na Groblach 22 ☎ 12 426 2625

PURO

purohotel.pl

This funkily sophisticated glass cube near the main station and Krakowska mall has retro-styled public spaces but 21st-century rooms. The color schemes are cool but relaxing and there are useful extras like free WiFi in the rooms, free international phone calls and underground parking.

🔲 J2 🔲 ul. Ogrodowa 10 ☎ 12 314 2100

RADISSON BLU KRAKOW

radissonblu.com

In an elegant building next to the Philharmonic Hall, the Radisson is geared to business travelers. Amenities include air-conditioning, underground parking, 24-hour room service, gym and sauna. On-site eating options include an international and a Polish restaurant, and the Salt&Co café-bar with salt walls.

🔲 H4 🔲 ul. Straszewskiego 17 ☎ 12 618 8888

PRICING

It seems to be a near-universal practice for hotels in Krakow to charge a rate for the room regardless of how many people are staying in it. Also be aware that some hotels include breakfast in their room rates and others do not.

Luxury Hotels

PRICES

Expect to pay over 500PLN (€150) a night for a double room in a luxury hotel.

HOTEL COPERNICUS
hotel.com.pl

On Krakow's most historic street under Wawel Hill, this hotel has a 14th-century facade yet all the modern features you might want, including a small pool in the Gothic cellars, a roof terrace, air conditioning, and the relaxed feel and decor of a boutique hotel. The 29 rooms have friezes fit for a Renaissance prince, beamed ceilings and restored fragments of medieval wall painting.

✚ H5 ✉ ul. Kanonicza 16 ☎ 12 424 3400

HOTEL GRÓDEK
donimirski.com

A sympathetically restored former palace with 23 rooms in a quiet spot next to a Dominican convent, the Gródek is a short walk from the main market square. Each room is individually decorated, but all have air conditioning and up-to-date bathrooms paired with antique-style furniture. The hotel has its own archaeological museum containing finds made during the conversion of the 16th-century building.

✚ J4 ✉ ul. Na Gródku 4 ☎ 12 431 9030

HOTEL MALTAŃSKI
donimirski.com

This is a true boutique hotel in green surroundings on the edge of the Planty, near the Franciscan Church in the Old Town. In a complex of three low, white buildings full of character and as rich in history as any in Krakow (the names Lubomirski, Czartoryski and Potocki feature), the 16 pretty rooms don't disappoint. Good facilities include free WiFi in all rooms and guarded parking.

✚ H5 ✉ ul. Straszewskiego 4 ☎ 12 431 0010

HOTEL STARY
stary.hotel.com.pl

Named for the Stary Theater nearby, this chic hotel has been converted from an ancient building in the Old Town. Some of the 53 rooms are contemporary, others more historical with original frescoes. The vaulted cellars house two pools, a fitness center, and a health-giving salt cave. There is a rooftop restaurant and a café-bar with views of the Mariacki church.

✚ H3 ✉ ul. Szczepańska 5 ☎ 12 384 0808

OSTOYA PALACE HOTEL
ostoyapalace.pl

In a romantic 19th-century building just outside the Planty, the 24 rooms have old doors, parquet floors and traditional tiled stoves, but also air conditioning and showers rather than tubs, though one suite has a whirlpool bath. There's an on-site restaurant too.

✚ G4 ✉ ul. Piłsudskiego 24 ☎ 12 430 9000

POD RÓŻĄ
hotel.com.pl

The oldest hotel in the city dates back to the 17th century. Its motto is "Let this house last as long as an ant does not drink all the water from the seas and a tortoise walk around the whole world." Franz Liszt and Tsar Alexander I both stayed here, "Under the Sign of the Rose," on the Royal Route. The 57 rooms have marble bathrooms and heated floors, yet original frescoes remain. There's also a gym with rooftop views.

✚ J3 ✉ ul. Floriańska 14 ☎ 12 424 3300

Krakow is a relaxed, well-organized, fun city. Once you've arrived from the airport you will be able to walk almost everywhere you want to go, but if you do use public transport, you'll find it is safe, clean and punctual, and the locals are helpful.

Planning Ahead **114**
Getting There **116**
Getting Around **118**
Essential Facts **120**
Language **122**
Timeline **124**

Planning Ahead

When to Go

Krakow has a temperate climate with frequent changes in the weather. Carry an umbrella and something warm. May and June tend to be best—the weather is good and the city buzzes with festivals. Summer is busy; winter days are cold but the Christmas market is in town.

AVERAGE DAILY MAXIMUM TEMPERATURES

JAN	FEB	MAR	APR	MAY	JUN	JUL	AUG	SEP	OCT	NOV	DEC
33°F	37°F	46°F	56°F	67°F	71°F	74°F	74°F	65°F	56°F	43°F	36°F
1°C	3°C	8°C	13°C	19°C	22°C	23°C	23°C	18°C	13°C	6°C	2°C

Spring (Mar–Apr) Very variable, with showers and sun by turns.
Summer (May–August) Hot but western winds bring storms and rain.
Autumn (Sep–Oct) Variable but can be dry, sunny and crisp with golden days.
Winter (Nov–Feb) Eastern winds mean less rain, but the cold can be penetrating and it can snow, particularly in January.

WHAT'S ON

January Carnival season.
February Processions of the hooded Brothers of the Good Death at the Franciscan Church every Fri in Lent. *International Sea Shanty Festival.*
March/April *Misteria Paschalia* music festival. Holy Week and Good Friday services. *Bach Days* music festival.
May Polish Flag Day. Constitution Day. *Cracovia Marathon. St. Stanisław* procession: Wawel to Skałka. *Corpus Christi*: procession with scattering of flower petals. *Cracow Screen Festival. Juwenalia* student festival. *Night of Museums:*

special events. *Lajkonik parade* (Thu after Corpus Christi). *Film Music Festival.* Photography month: exhibitions citywide.
June *Krakow Festival. Children's Day. Open Gardens Festival.* Pageant to enthrone the cockerel king of the Brotherhood of Riflemen. *Wianki* festival: floating wreaths with candles on the Vistula, all-night merrymaking, music and fireworks. *Grand Dragon Parade.*
July Festivals of Jewish culture, military bands, jazz, Carpathian music.
August Folk festival. *Pierogi* food festival.

September *Sacrum Profanum* festival of contemporary music.
October Month of *Encounters with Jewish Culture, Organ Music Days, Krakow Book Fair.*
November All Saints' Day and All Souls' Day: flowers and candles put on graves. Independence Day. Krakow's Christmas market opens on Rynek Główny. *Zaduszki* jazz festival
December Feast of *Mikołaj*: St. Nicholas brings children gifts. Christmas cribs on show (morning of first Thursday in December) in Rynek Główny. *Sylwester*: New Year's Eve celebrations.

Krakow Online

krakow.pl
The city government site is an invaluable source of information. It includes an official accommodations booking system and comprehensive listings for theaters, cinemas, galleries and other cultural centers.

biurofestiwalowe.pl
Krakow's Festival Office coordinates the plethora of events and festivals in the city. This is a useful resource for finding the dates of the many movable feasts.

mhk.pl
The website of the Historical Museum of the City of Krakow should be your first stop for information about Krakow's main attractions. It not only details what's on in all its many branches but also helps you decode the sometimes byzantine opening times.

mnk.pl
The official website of the National Museum covers the many museums run by the state, not the city—which include the Czartoryski Museum, the Szołayskich House, the Mehoffer House and the Erazm Ciołek Palace as well as the main museum.

karnet.krakow.pl
The official listings guide is more useful to you if your interests turn toward art and Chopin rather than Irish pubs and death metal.

krakow-info.com
This is similar to the other listings sites, but worth looking at for its handy hints pages, pages of background information, FAQs and tips for visitors with disabilities.

poland.travel
The official site of the Polish National Tourist Office is useful for background information and planning trips farther afield.

TRAVEL SITES

mcit.pl
Tourist Information service for Małopolska, the region around Krakow, which organizes tours from its office at ul. Grodzka 31.

zakopane-life.com
Listings and information helpful for anyone traveling south to the mountains.

fodors.com
A complete travel-planning site. You can research prices and weather; book air tickets, cars and rooms; ask questions (and get answers) from fellow travelers.

INTERNET ACCESS

As in most Western cities, it is easy to access the internet in Krakow via your phone or laptop. Every café, hotel and restaurant has WiFi, as do the Rynek Głowny and the center of Kazimierz.

NEED TO KNOW PLANNING AHEAD

Getting There

Poland is within the 26-state Schengen Agreement area and no visa is required for citizens of other Schengen countries. There's no limit to how long other EU nationals can stay, but passport holders from the US, Canada, Australia and New Zealand will need a visa for a visit longer than 90 days. In certain circumstances visitors from those countries who do not hold full passports will need a visa; visitors from other countries may also need one. Check before traveling on the Polish Ministry of Foreign Affairs website at msz.gov.pl. Medical care is good in Krakow but you will need adequate travel insurance. Although EU citizens can use an EHIC card, it is not wise to rely solely on this.

TIPS

● If traveling to or from Krakow by train, check out the excellent seat61.com website, which has lots of tips.

● Luggage with wheels is handy in Krakow. It is easy to get from the train or the bus station into the center of the Old Town using the wide, ramped underpass.

AIRPORTS

There are direct flights to Krakow from Europe and North America into Krakow's John Paul II International Airport (also known as Krakow-Balice) which also receives many charter flights.

John Paul II International Airport

15km (9 miles)

10km (6 miles)

5km (3 miles)

● Central Krakow

FROM THE AIRPORT

All flights arrive at Krakow's John Paul II International Airport (1 ul. kpt. Medweckiego, Balice, tel 0801 055 000, krakowairport.pl), about 12km (8 miles) from the city center. In the international terminal you will find tourist information, facilities for visitors with disabilities, mother and baby rooms, foreign exchange facilities and ATMs, a bank (Mon–Fri 8–8, Sat–Sun 9.15–8), a post office (Mon–Fri 8–2.45), shops and cafés and lost luggage (tel 12 285 5121). You'll also find desks for all the main car rental companies and a 24-hour car park (tel 12 639 3065 or 12 295 3178; the cost is 9PLN an hour, 49PLN a day).

Taxis are metered and will give you a receipt (paragon) if requested. Depending on traffic, it's a 20- to 30-minute drive to the Old Town that will cost 60–120PLN. To call the airport's official taxi company, dial 12 258 0258. Your hotel or hostel may well offer to send a car to meet you and this may prove to be slightly cheaper.

Buses 208 and 292 leave from a stop just past the train shuttle bus stop—turn right on

leaving the international terminal. Not very frequent (departures are about 40 minutes apart), they stop everywhere on the way into the city and take the better part of an hour to get to the main station. A ticket machine at the stop takes coins and has ticket information in English. A kiosk upstairs in the international terminal also sells bus tickets or you can pay the driver. One-way tickets are 4PLN.

The best option is the fast and efficient train from the airport to the city's main station (Dworzec Główny). The whole journey takes about 20 minutes but at the time of writing they leave only once an hour due to works on the tracks. You can buy tickets (9PLN) on the train or before boarding.

BY BUS

The main bus terminal is next to the main train station and has an entrance from ul. Bosacka. There's a helpful English-language version of its website, rda.krakow.pl, with departure times and a ticket sales portal. The international ticket office at the terminal is open daily 7am–7.45pm (tel 12 393 5255). Eurolines runs international buses to Krakow from many European cities. For details of routes, tickets and 15- and 30-day European passes see its website (eurolines.com). Its partner company in Poland is Arriva Eurolines Polska (tel 703 303 333, arrivabus.pl).

BY RAIL

Trains from the airport, from other parts of Poland and the rest of Europe arrive and depart from the main station, Dworzec Główny, just outside the Planty and the Old Town. There are left-luggage facilities. The express to Warsaw takes about two and a half hours and you must buy your tickets in advance. Useful websites for rail travel within Poland are rozklad-pkp. pl and intercity.pl. For express services and trains into and out of Poland, see polrail.com. There are direct trains to Krakow from Prague, Budapest and Vienna.

DEPARTURES

● On leaving Krakow by train for the airport, be aware that if you buy a ticket in advance it will be timed and will be valid for only two hours after the time it is issued. It's also quite a long walk from the station entrance and the ticket office to the departure platform for the airport train, so leave yourself plenty of time.

● Security at Krakow-Balice airport is very strict. You will not be allowed to take any container larger than 100ml through security in your hand luggage. This covers everything from full bottles of vodka to empty crystal vases. You'll need a permit to export anything made before 1945 (details on poland.travel).

DRIVING

It's only worth driving to Krakow if your visit to the city is part of a longer road journey in Europe. The main international motorways serving Krakow are the A4 (from Germany through Wrocław, Katowice, Krakow, Tarnów and Rzeszów into the Ukraine) and the A7 from Gdańsk through Warsaw and Krakow to Slovakia.

Getting Around

The Krakow Card (2-day 100PLN; 3-day 120PLN; krakowcard.com) gives you free travel on city buses and trams day and night, including transport to the airport and Wieliczka Salt Mines, and free entry to 40 of Krakow's museums, as well as discounts in shops and restaurants. It's sold in tourist information centers and many hotels, or can be bought in advance online.

The bus and tram map of Krakow is often under revision because of frequent roadworks in the Old Town and road improvements necessitating closures in the rest of the city. Up-to-date bus and tram maps on paper do not exist and those on websites are difficult to read. However, you will find tourist information offices, hotel receptionists and local people helpful. At the larger stops, such as the green wooden bus shelter opposite the main MPK office on ul. Podwale, staff will be able to tell you how to get to your destination.

ON TWO FEET

The best way to see Krakow is to walk. It's a compact, mainly flat city and on a short visit you'll scarcely need to use public transport if you are staying in the Old Town or Kazimierz. Many companies run walking tours, which are a good way of orienting yourself. There is a huge variety of these in Krakow, catering to all tastes. Krakow Daily Walks is one of the most popular (meet in front of the Tourist Information Office, at plac Mariacki 3, tel 12 430 2117, krakow-travel.com, costing 50PLN) for the Old Town walk.

BUSES AND TRAMS

The city-run buses and trams operate a good service including night buses in and around Krakow (see mpk.krakow.pl). Buy tickets from machines at bus and tram stops (these usually give change but don't take notes), nearby kiosks, and machines on some of the newer buses. The ticket machines have information in English too. If you buy a ticket on board from the driver you will have to pay a supplement of 0.50PLN. There are also higher rates for buses operating within the larger metropolitan area.

Buses and trams operate a flat-fare system within the city boundaries:

● 3.80PLN for single ticket
● 5PLN for a 60-minute ticket (useful for journeys involving two buses or a bus and a tram, such as from the center to Kopiec Kościuszko)
● 15PLN for a 24-hour ticket (good if you are planning on taking a night bus or two)
● 24PLN for a 48-hour ticket
● 36PLN for a 72-hour ticket
● 48PLN for a weekly ticket.

Reduced-price tickets are available for children, senior citizens and family (for example, a family weekend ticket costs 16PLN).

Validate your ticket on boarding by punching it in one of the orange machines near the door and keep it in case of inspection.

MINIBUSES

You will see minibuses zipping about on various main streets around the Planty and particularly from the Old Town down to Podgórze or Kazimierz and out to Wieliczka. These are private enterprises but regulated. The destination is shown on the front and you pay the driver or sometimes there is a conductor. Fares vary but are roughly double those on official city buses. Most begin at ul. Pawia near the main railway station. They can seem a bit daunting to non-Polish-speaking visitors but many tourists use them.

TAXIS

Use only metered taxis, which are clearly marked. Charges are moderate, like most things in Krakow. There are handy taxi ranks just within the Planty at Plac Szczepański, ul. Sienna and ul. Sławkowska, and also at the junction of ul. Stradomska and ul. Bernardyńska.

To call for a taxi, try Radio Taxi Wawel on 12 266 6666 or 19666 from your cell; Mega Taxi on 12 400 0000 or 12 19625; Partner Taxi on 12 19633; or Barbakan Taxi on 12 19661 or at barbakan.krakow.pl (the website has an English version). Certain fleets will offer a 10 percent reduction for those who book by telephone.

VISITORS WITH DISABILITIES

Krakow is a wonderfully well-preserved medieval city and many premises are prevented by their historic nature from installing as many facilities for visitors with disabilities as they might like. Since the mid-1990s Poland has required all new public buildings to have wheelchair access. This law also applies to the refurbishment of older buildings. The city restoration schedule means many but not yet all of Krakow's museums now have ramps and elevators.

Contact the Galeria Stańczyk information center for visitors with disabilities (ul. Królewska 94, tel 12 636 8584, open Tue, Thu 11–5).

OFFBEAT TOURS

● Insiders Creative Tours by car or on foot offer their own perspective on Essential Krakow, Criminal Krakow, Women of Krakow and the completely wacky Night Taxi—a hilarious and intriguing tour led by "Professor Vodka." From 70PLN per person ☎ 12 421 4835, krakow-tours.info.

● Communism Tours by Crazy Guides take you around Nowa Huta in a Soviet-era Trabant or out to an old-fashioned farm for dinner. From 119PLN per person ☎ 500 091 200, crazyguides.com

CITY CYCLING

As a flat city with many students, Krakow is full of cyclists, bike rental firms and bike tours.

● Cool Tour Company city bikes, tandems, recumbent bikes and penny farthings cost from 6PLN an hour. They also offer bike tours by day and night ✉ Courtyard, ul. Grodzka 2 ☎ 12 430 2034, cooltourcompany.com

● Cruising Krakow city and country tours cost from 75PLN and bike rentals from 15PLN for three hours ✉ ul. Basztowa 17 ☎ 12 265 81057, 514 556 017, cruisingkrakow.com

Essential Facts

The złoty is the official currency in Poland, abbreviated to zł. or PLN. There are 100 groszy (gr.) in one złoty. Banknotes come in denominations of 10, 20, 50, 100 and 200 złotych; coins as 1 złoty, 2 złote and 5 złotych, 50, 20, 10, 5 groszy, 2 grosze and 1 grosz.

EMBASSIES AND CONSULATES

● **British Honorary Consulate** ✉ ul. św. Anny 9 ☎ 12 421 7030, gov.uk ⏰ Mon–Fri 9–3
● **US Consulate General** ✉ ul. Stolarska 9 ☎ 12 424 5100, krakow.usconsulate.gov ⏰ Mon–Fri 8.30–3
● **Candian Embassy** ✉ ul. Jana Matejki 1/5, Warsaw ☎ 22 584 3100, poland.gc.ca ⏰ Mon–Fri 8.30–4.30
● **Irish Embassy** ✉ ul. Mysia 5, Warsaw ☎ 22 849 6633, embassyofireland.pl ⏰ Mon–Fri 9–1, 2–5
● **Spanish Embassy** ✉ ul. Myśliwiecka 5, Warsaw ☎ 22 584 3000, exteriores.gob.es ⏰ Mon–Fri 8.30–4
● **Portuguese Embassy** ✉ ul. Ateńska 37, Warsaw ☎ 22 511 1010, ambasada-portugalii.pl ⏰ Mon–Fri 9–3

ELECTRICITY

In common with the rest of Europe, Poland has a 220-volt electrical system and uses two-round-pin plugs.

LOST PROPERTY

Try the local government Biuro Rzeczy Znalezionych at ul. Wielicka 28, office 114, tel 12 616 5713. For lost property on public transportation, tel 12 254 1150.

MEDICAL TREATMENT

For minor ailments, try a pharmacy (*apteka*) first. Many speak English.
● For 24-hour medical information, tel 12 661 2240
● For 24-hour private medical services, try Scanmed, tel 12 629 8800; or Medicover, tel 500 900 500
● For ambulance service, tel 999 or 112 (general emergency number) from a cellphone

MONEY

Bank cards are widely accepted and there are many cashpoint machines (ATMs), especially in the main tourist areas, with several in the Rynek Główny and in the main streets of the Old Town. Compare the bank rate of exchange with that of one of the many foreign exchange bureaux *(kantor)* before changing your money—you may find a better rate. Do not change money with anyone in the street. On entering the European Union, Poland pledged to adopt the euro but no date has been set and there is considerable internal opposition to it.

OPENING HOURS

Shops choose their own opening hours. In general this is Mon–Fri 10–6 or 7, with earlier closing on Saturday. Within the Planty and around Kazimierz shops are often open on Sunday too. Grocery and food shops open earlier and stay open later. There are many small 24-hour supermarkets in the Old Town, especially on the inner edge of the Planty. Even

beyond the Planty, convenience stores stay open 7am–11pm or midnight. Most museums are closed on Mondays. Banks are generally open Mon–Fri 8–5, Sat 8–1.

POST
Some of the assistants at the main post office speak English (Poczta Główna, ul. Westerplatte 20, Mon–Fri 7.30am–8.30pm, Sat 8–2). You can also buy stamps at kiosks. Postboxes are red with a symbol of a yellow horn in a blue disc and the legend Poczta Polska.

PUBLIC HOLIDAYS
- Jan 1 (New Year's Day)
- May 1 (Labor Day), May 3 (Constitution Day)
- Ascension Day (40 days after Easter)
- Feast of Corpus Christi (Thursday after Trinity Sunday, which is 60 days after Easter)
- Aug 15 (Feast of the Assumption)
- Nov 1 (All Saints' Day), Nov 11 (Independence Day)
- Dec 25, Dec 26 (Christmas)

TOILETS
A triangle often designates male toilets *(męski)*; a circle women's *(damski)*. Public toilets and many cafés charge 1–5PLN to use the facilities.

TOURIST INFORMATION
City Tourist Information Network (krakow.pl):
- Town Hall Tower, Rynek Główny 1, tel 12 433 7310, open daily 9–7
- International Airport Krakow-Balice, tel 12 285 5341, open daily 9–7
- ul. Szpitalna 25, tel 12 432 0110, open daily 9–7
- ul. św. Jana 2, tel 12 421 7787, open daily 10–6
- ul. Józefa 7, tel 12 422 0471, open daily 10–5
- CORT, ul. Powiśle 11, tel 513 099 688, open daily 9–7
- Wyspiański 2000 Pavilion, pl. Wszystkich Świętych 2, tel 12 616 1886, open daily 9–7

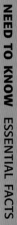

NEED TO KNOW ESSENTIAL FACTS

Language

In Polish every letter is pronounced and the stress is almost always on the penultimate syllable. Ą is a nasal "on," while ę is also nasal. Say i as in the English "me." The vowel y is gutteral as in "myth;" j provides the English y sound as in "yeah;" ó and u are as in the English "cool." English l and w sounds to get ł. The letter c is like ts in "bits;" g is as in "get;" r is rolled; ń is a softer n with a "ye" aftertaste and ź is like the French j in "journal." Certain pairs of letters are said as one sound: ch, like the Polish h, is hard as in the Scottish "loch;" cz is like English ch in "church;" ś and sz like English sh as in "shed;" rz as Polish ż, like English s in "leisure."

USEFUL WORDS

yes	*tak*
no	*nie*
please	*proszę*
thank you	*dziękuję*
you're welcome	*proszę bardzo*
excuse me/I'm sorry	*przepraszam*
where?	*gdzie?*
here	*tu, tutaj*
there	*tam*
when?	*kiedy?*
now	*teraz*
later	*później*
why?	*dlaczego?*
who?	*kto?*
May I? Can I...?	*Czy mogę...?*
good morning/ good afternoon	*dzień dobry*
good evening	*dobry wieczór*
good night	*dobranoc*
goodbye	*do widzenia/do*
bye	*zobaczenia*
hi, hello	*cześć*
left/on the left	*po lewej/na lewo*
right/on the right	*po prawej/na prawo*
open	*otwarty/czynny (shops)*
closed	*zamknięty/nieczynny (shops)*
today	*dzisiaj/dziś*
tomorrow	*jutro*
later	*potem*

DAYS OF THE WEEK

Monday	*poniedziałek*
Tuesday	*wtorek*
Wednesday	*środa*
Thursday	*czwartek*
Friday	*piątek*
Saturday	*sobota*
Sunday	*niedziela*

MONTHS

January	*styczeń*
February	*luty*
March	*marzec*
Apri	*kwiecień*
May	*maj*
June	*czerwiec*
July	*lipiec*
August	*sierpień*
September	*wrzesień*
October	*październik*
November	*listopad*
December	*grudzień*

SEASONS

Spring	*wiosna*
Summer	*lato*
Autumn	*jesień*
Winter	*zima*

EMERGENCIES

Help!	*Pomocy!*
Stop, thief!	*Lapać złodzieja*
Can you help me, please?	*Proszę o pomoc?*
Call the police	*Proszę zawołać policję*
Call an ambulance	*Proszę zadzwonić po pogotowie*
I have lost my wallet	*Zgubiłem portmonetkę*
I have lost my passport	*Zgubiłem paszporta*
Where is the police station?	*Gdzie jest komisariat policji?*
Where is the hospital?	*Gdzie jest szpital?*
I don't feel well	*Źle się czuję*
first aid	*pierwsza pomoc*

NUMBERS

1	*jeden*
2	*dwa/dwie*
3	*trzy*
4	*cztery*
5	*pięć*
6	*sześć*
7	*siedem*
8	*osiem*
9	*dziewięć*
10	*dziesięć*
20	*dwadzieścia*
30	*trzydzieści*
40	*czterdzieści*
50	*pięćdziesiąt*
100	*sto*
1,000	*tysiąc*

USEFUL PHRASES

How are you? (formal)	*Jak się pan/pani miewa?*
Very well, thanks	*Bardzo dobrze, dziękuję*
How are you? (informal)	*Jak sie masz?*
I'm fine	*U mnie w porządku*
I do not understand	*Nie rozumiem*
How much is it?	*Ile to kosztuje?*
Do you have a room?	*Czy pan/pani ma pokój?*
How much per night?	*Ile kosztuje za dobę?* (doba means a night and a day)
with bath/shower	*z łazienką/z przysznicem*
When is breakfast served?	*O której godzinie jest śniadanie?*
Where is the train/bus station?	*Gdzie dworzec/dworzec autobusowy?*
Where are we?	*Gdzie jesteśmy?*
Do I have to get off here?	*Czy to mój przystanek?*
I'm looking for…	*Szukam…*
Where can I buy…?	*Gdzie można kupić…?*
A table for… please	*Proszę stolik dla…*
The bill, please?	*Proszę rachunek*
We didn't have this	*Nie jedliśmy tego*
Where are the restrooms?	*Gdzie są toalety?*

Timeline

CULTURED CAPITAL

Between the 11th and 17th centuries Krakow was the capital of Poland but even when the country disappeared entirely under the partitions of the 18th and 19th centuries the city remained an artistic and intellectual powerhouse as part of the province of Galicia, which stretched in a crescent east from Krakow through to present-day Ukraine.

c.50,000 BC Evidence of settlers on Wawel Hill.

7th-8th century AD Era of legendary founder King Krak and his daughter Wanda.

965 First written record of Krakow by Ibrahim ibn Jacub, a merchant from Cordoba.

c. 1038 Kazimierz I (the Restorer) declares Krakow capital of Poland.

1257 Krakow city charter granted by Duke Bolesław the Chaste.

1364 Krakow Academy, forerunner of the Jagiellonian University, founded by Kazimierz III, the Great.

1386 Child bride Queen Jadwiga of Poland marries Grand Duke Władysław Jagiełło, Grand Duke of Lithuania, joining the two countries.

1596 King Zygmunt III moves Polish court from Krakow to Warsaw.

1655–57 First invasion of Krakow by Swedish forces.

1772 First of three partitions of Poland between Austria, Prussia and Russia. Krakow under Austrian occupation.

1793 Krakow under Russian occupation after second partition.

From left: Władysław Jagiełło statue; Poles fleeing their country in 1939; Zygmunt's Column in Warsaw; Lech Wałęsa, the trade union activist and politician; Pope John Paul II

1795 Krakow becomes part of Austria after third Polish partition. The country of Poland ceases to exist.

1850 The Great Fire razes half the city.

1918 Poland regains independence after 123 years of foreign occupation.

1939 Nazis occupy Krakow on September 6.

1941 Krakow's Jews evicted from their homes and taken to the new ghetto at Podgórze.

1943 Liquidation of the Podgórze ghetto.

1945 Red Army enters Krakow.

1949 Construction of the Socialist-Realist district of Nowa Huta begins.

1978 Krakow put on Unesco World Heritage List; Cardinal Karol Wojtyła, Archbishop of Krakow, elected Pope John Paul II.

1990 Solidarity leader Lech Wałęsa elected President of Poland after fall of Communism.

2004 Poland joins European Union.

2015 Poland marks 70 years since the liberation of Auschwitz.

2018 Tradition of making Christmas cribs (*szopki*) added to Unesco Cultural Heritage list.

QUEEN, KING, SAINT

Queen Jadwiga was all three. As a girl, she rejected her lover in favor of a marriage that would be politically advantageous for the country she was to rule. One of two queens of Poland who was also crowned king, she was canonized by Pope John Paul II at a Mass on Błonia Fields in 1997.

CROWNED HEADS

Even after the capital moved to Warsaw, the kings of Poland continued to be crowned at Krakow's Wawel Cathedral. The crypt is still the resting place of Poland's heroes to this day.

Index

A

accommodations 18, 108–112
air travel 116–117
amber 10, 36
Apteka Pod Orłem 92–93
Aqua Park 106
Archdiocesan Museum 50
art galleries, commercial 82
arts and crafts 11, 12, 56
ATMs 120
Auschwitz-Birkenau 8, 16,
    100–101

B

banks 120
Barbakan 51
Beyond the Planty 85–96
    map 86–87
    sights 88–95
    where to eat 96
bike rental 119
Bishop Erazm Ciołek's Palace
    9, 50
Błonia fields 16, 94
Botanical Gardens 16, 95
Brama Floriańska 50
buses
    city 118–119
    international 117
    minibuses 119

C

cabaret 33
cafés 18, 44
Celestat 94
Centre for Jewish Culture 83
Christmas Market 11
Church on the Rock 94–95
cinemas 57
classical music 16, 37, 57,
    83, 114
climate and seasons 114
Cloth Hall 8, 30–31
Collegium Maius 8, 42–43
Collegium Novum 51
Copernicus, Nicholas 43, 54
Corpus Christi Church 78
currency exchange 120
cycling 119
Czartoryski Museum 9,
    48–49
Częstochowa 105

D

disabilities, visitors with 119
dorożki 32
Dragon's Lair 8, 66
dragon symbol 8, 66
driving 117

E

eating out 14–15
    barbecues 68
    Jewish cuisine 84
    mealtimes 14
    Polish cuisine 15, 38
    street food 11, 82
    traditional drinks 37
    where to eat 14
electricity 120
embassies and consulates
    121
emergency telephone numbers
    120
entertainment and nightlife
    13, 16–17
    Farther Afield 106
    Kazimierz 83
    Rynek Główny 37
    Within the Planty 57
Ethnographic Museum 9,
    72–73
excursions 105
    Częstochowa 105
    Zakopane 105

F

Farther Afield 97–106
    entertainment and nightlife
        106
    excursions 105
    map 98–99
    sights 100–104
    where to eat 106
festivals and events 114
Florian's Gate 51
fortifications 67
Franciscan Church 9, 46–47

G

Galicia Jewish Museum
    8, 18, 77
ghetto 92–93
glass and crystal 12, 36, 56
golf 106

H

hejnał 8, 24
High Synagogue 79
Historical Museum of the
    City of Krakow 28
history 124–125
horse-drawn cabs 32
hostels 18, 109
hotels 18, 108–112

I

insurance 116
internet access 110, 115

J

Jama Michalika 9, 44
Jasna Góra 105
jazz 17, 37, 57
jewelry 10, 12, 36, 56, 82
John Paul II, Pope 5, 45, 54,
    94, 125
John Paul II Centre 49
Judaica Foundation 83

K

Kamienica Hipolitów 32
Kamienica Szołayskich 9, 45
Kamienice 9, 25
Katedra Wawelska 9, 18, 62–63
Katyń 16, 52
Kazimierz 4, 69–84
    entertainment and nightlife
        83
    map 70–71
    shopping 82
    sights 72–79
    walk 81
    where to eat 84
klezmer music 18, 74, 83
Kopalnia Soli Wieliczka
    9, 102–103
Kopiec Kościuszki 104
Kościół św. Andrzeja 18, 51–52
Kościół św. Anny 52
Kościół św. Barbary 32
Kościół Bożego Ciała 78
Kościół Franciszkanów 9, 45
Kościół św. Idziego 53
Kościół św. Katarzyny 95
Kościół Mariacki 9, 18, 24,
    26–27
Kościół Paulinów na Skałce
    94–95
Kościół Pijarów 51–52
Kościół św. Piotra i Pawła 16, 52
Kościół św. Wojciecha 17, 33
Kościuszko, Tadeusz 63, 67, 104
Kościuszko Mound 17, 104
Krakow Zoo 16, 104, 106
Krzysztofory Palace 8, 28
Krzyż Katyński 53

L

Lajkonik 5
language 122–123
Las Wolski 104
lost property 120
Lost Wawel exhibition 67

M

Manga Japanese Center 17, 95
markets 82
Marksmen's Guild 94

medical treatment 120
Mehoffer, Józef 88–89
Mickiewicz, Adam 33, 63
money 120
Museum of Art of Old Poland 50
Museum of the Jagiellonian University 8, 42–43
museum opening hours 120
Museum of Urban Engineering 78
Muzeum Archeologiczne 53
Muzeum Dom Mehoffera 9, 88–89
Muzeum Etnograficzne 9, 72–73
Muzeum Farmacji 53
Muzeum Inżynierii Miejskiej 78
Muzeum Książąt Czatoryskich 9, 46–47
Muzeum Narodowe w Krakowie 9, 90–91
Muzeum Sztuki i Techniki Japońskiej Manggha 17, 95

N
National Museum 9, 90–91
New Jewish Cemetery 78
nightlife see entertainment and nightlife
Nowa Huta 104
Nowy Cmentarz Żydowski 78

O
Ogród Botaniczny 16, 95
Old Synagogue 8, 75
Old Theater 54
opening hours 120
opera 57

P
Pałac Biskupa Ezrama Ciołka 9, 50
Pałac Biskupi 54
Pałac Królewski na Wawelu 9, 64–65
Pałac Krzysztofory 8, 28
Park Jordana 16, 94
passports and visas 116
pharmacies 120
Pharmacy Museum 53
Piarist Church 52
Piwnica Pod Baranami 33
Plac Nowy 8, 74, 82
Planty see Within the Planty
police 121
Pomnik Adama Mickiewicza 33
Pomnik Kopernika 54
Pomnik Kościuszki 67

Pomnik Piotra Skrzyneckiego 34
postal services 121
public holidays 121

R
Remuh Synagogue and Cemetery 8, 76
Restauracja Wierzynek 8, 29
Rynek Główny 20–38
    entertainment and nightlife 37
    map 22–23
    shopping 36
    sights 24–34
    walk 35
    where to eat 38

S
St. Adalbert's Church 17, 33
St. Andrew's Church 18, 51–52
St. Anne's Church 52
St. Barbara's Church 32
St. Catherine's Church 95
St. Giles's Church 53
St. Mary's Church 9, 18, 24, 26–27
salt mines 9, 102–103
Schindler's Krakow 8, 92–93
shopping 10–12
    Kazimierz 82
    opening hours 120
    Rynek Główny 36
    shopping malls 10, 82
    Within the Planty 56
sightseeing tours 118, 119
skiing 105
Skrzynecki, Piotr 34
Slowacki Theater 16, 17, 54
Smocza Jama 8, 66
SS Peter and Paul 16, 52
Stara Synagoga 8, 75
Stary Teatr 54
Sukiennice 8, 30–31
Sukiennice Gallery 31
Synagoga i Cmentarz Remuh 8, 76
Synagoga Izaaka 79
Synagoga Tempel 79
Synagoga Wysoka 79

T
Tatra National Park 105
taxis 119
Teatr im Juliusza Słowackiego 16, 17, 54
time differences 114
tipping 14
toilets 121
Tourist Card 118

tourist information 115, 121
Town Hall Tower 17, 34
train services 116, 117
two-day itinerary 6–7

U
Ulica Pomorska 16, 95
Ulica Szeroka 79

V
vodka 11, 13

W
walking tours 118
walks
    Kazimierz 81
    Rynek Główny 35
    Within the Planty 55
Wawel Castle 9, 64–65
Wawel Cathedral 9, 18, 62–63
Wawel Hill 59–68
    map 60–61
    where to eat 68
    sights 62–67
Wawel Zaginiony 67
websites 115
where to eat 15
    Beyond the Planty 96
    Farther Afield 106
    Kazimierz 84
    Rynek Główny 38
    Wawel Hill 68
    Within the Planty 58
Wieża Ratuszowa 34
Within the Planty 16, 39–58
    entertainment and nightlife 57
    map 40–41
    shopping 56
    sights 42–54
    walk 55
    where to eat 58
Wyspiański Museum 45

Z
Zakopane 105
Żydowskie Muzeum Galicja 8, 18, 77

Krakow 25 Best

WRITTEN BY Renata Rubnikowicz
UPDATED BY Dorota Wąsik
SERIES EDITOR Clare Ashton
COVER DESIGN Jessica Gonzalez
DESIGN WORK Liz Baldin
COLOR REPROGRAPHICS Ian Little

Published in the United Kingdom by AA Publishing.

ISBN 978-1-6409-7202-5

SECOND EDITION

Printed and bound in China by 1010 Printing Group Limited

10 9 8 7 6 5 4 3 2 1

A05671
Mapping data supplied by Global Mapping, Brackley, UK © Global Mapping and data available from openstreetmap.org © under the Open Database License found at opendatacommons.org
Transport map © Communicarta Ltd, UK

We would like to thank the following photographers, companies and picture libraries for their assistance in the preparation of this book.

All images copyright AA/A Mockford & N Bonett, except:

14tcr Chata Restaurant; 18tr Max Jourdan; 18tcr Copernicus Hotel; 31 M Lanng; 32bl eFesenko/Alamy Stock Photo; 42t Arco Images GmbH/Alamy Stock Photo; 42–43 M Lanng; 50tl Witold Skrypczak/Alamy Stock Photo; 50tr AA World Travel Library/Alamy Stock Photo; 62tl Katedry na Wawelu; 63l Katedra na Wawelu; 66tr Eye Ubiquitous/Alamy Stock Photo; 72cl Muzeum Etnograficzne; 74tl AA/A Mockford & N Bonetti; 75tc Tomasz Kalarus; 77tr Zydowskie Museum Galicja; 90–91 Muzeum Narodowe w Krakowie; 97 Wieliczka Salt Mine archives; 100t AA/ James Tims; 100c AA/J Tims; 101tl AA/J Tims; 101tr AA/J Tims; 102tl AA/J Tims; 102–103 AA/J Tims; 102cl AA/J Tims; 102 Wieliczka Salt Mine archives; 103tr Wieliczka Salt Mine archives; 103cl AA/J Tims; 103cr AA/J Tims; 105 AA/J Tims; 106c AA/J Tims; 108tcr Hotel Copernicus; 124br Keystone/Getty Images; 125bl Polish National Tourist Office; 125bc Polish National Tourist Office; 125br Polish National Tourist Office.

Every effort has been made to trace the copyright holders, and we apologise in advance for any unintentional omissions or errors. We would be pleased to apply any corrections in a following edition of this publication.

Titles in the Series

- Amsterdam
- Bangkok
- Barcelona
- Berlin
- Boston
- Brussels and Bruges
- Budapest
- Chicago
- Dubai
- Dublin
- Edinburgh
- Florence
- Hong Kong
- Istanbul
- Krakow
- Las Vegas
- Lisbon
- London
- Madrid
- Melbourne
- Milan
- Montréal
- Munich
- New York City
- Orlando
- Paris
- Rome
- San Francisco
- Seattle
- Shanghai
- Singapore
- Sydney
- Tokyo
- Toronto
- Venice
- Vienna
- Washington, D.C.